RACHEL M

THE CIRCLE
OF LIFE

TEENAGE EDITION

A brilliant, practical guide on understanding
stress and how to build resilience,
self-confidence and happiness in teenagers.

References

The Art of being Brilliant – Andy Cope & Andy Whittaker

Youth Mental Health First Aid

Dr Robert Gonzalez, The Chopra Centre - p.24

*Youtube.com/user/MotivatingSuccess,*Famous Failures - p.51

Matthew Thorpe, MD, PHD published by Healthline

www.healthline.com, The Benefits of Meditation, page 94

FOREWORD

I have known Rachel for many years, and during that time I have had the privilege of seeing her mental health mission flourish as she's reached out to more and more young people.

Here in The Circus of Life she sets out in print the amazing work she's been doing to give teenagers the power and the confidence to take control of their lives and thrive in this crazy world – a world for which Rachel uses the apt analogy of the 'Big Top' where, whether we like it or not, we are all performers, 'juggling balls' and sometimes 'throwing knives'. She is the 'Ring Master' who gently guides, advises and reassures the reader like a trusted friend.

Rachel's experience of mental health issues within her own family – which she recounts with great candour and not an ounce of self-pity – informs much of what she writes in this book, so the reader knows immediately that it's truly authentic – the 'real deal'.

But this isn't a book looking back, it's a route map for life, a sparkling self-help manual for today's teenagers, many of whom find themselves struggling to navigate the choppy and sometimes hostile waters of 21st-Century adolescence.

What makes The Circus of Life so unique and so welcome is Rachel's characteristic emphasis on practical strategies for young people to manage their own mental health and to understand how their minds work, and what to do when they malfunction. Her writing truly empowers the reader and encourages them to 'Be [their] own life coach'.

Anyone who knows Rachel, or indeed anyone who has spent even a small amount of time with her, will testify to her passionate desire to help others, coupled magically with boundless charm and personal warmth – all of which you will discover with delight in this wonderful and necessary book.

Kendal Mills
Deputy Head (Pastoral),
Stamford School

Acknowledgements

To my wonderful husband. He has shown the patience of a saint and offered support beyond measure over the three years it has taken me to write this book. He is also the genius behind the imagery and design which has really brought the book to life.

I also want to thank my beautiful mum, my precious sons and my husband (again) for allowing me to share their stories.

A huge thank you must also go to my dad and my uncle for keeping me straight on grammar and spelling – without you it might of been a disastar!!!

Finally, a number of people that I have had the pleasure to work with in one capacity or another have inspired me along the way. These include: Tony Robbins, Positively MAD, Brian Mayne, Graham Cullen, MHFA, Faiy Rushton, Headspace.

CONTENTS

LIFE IS A CIRCUS
Enjoy the show!

My name is Rachel and I am a circus performer – just one of over 7 billion in this world.

You see, I believe that the world is a circus and we all need to learn the skills of performers to enjoy our time in the big top.

To begin with we are the clowns – falling over all the time, dribbling, making a mess, saying and doing funny things – this happens later in life too - much, much later!!

As we get older we need to master more demanding skills like:

- **juggling** – keeping many things on the go at one time
- **balancing** – we've all heard of work/life balance and this applies to kids, teenagers and adults in much the same way
- **walking the tightrope** – focussing on what's ahead, keeping our eye on the end goal even when things get a little wobbly
- **fire-eating** – dealing with danger, looking for excitement
- **performing** – like all acts in the circus: be proud of who you are, be proud of what you can do and don't be afraid to show it to the world

A successful circus performer dares to take risks, is fit and healthy, passionate about what they do and supportive to all around them – much like a successful human being.

This book is your introduction to the 'Circus of Life'. Step into the big top and let the show commence...

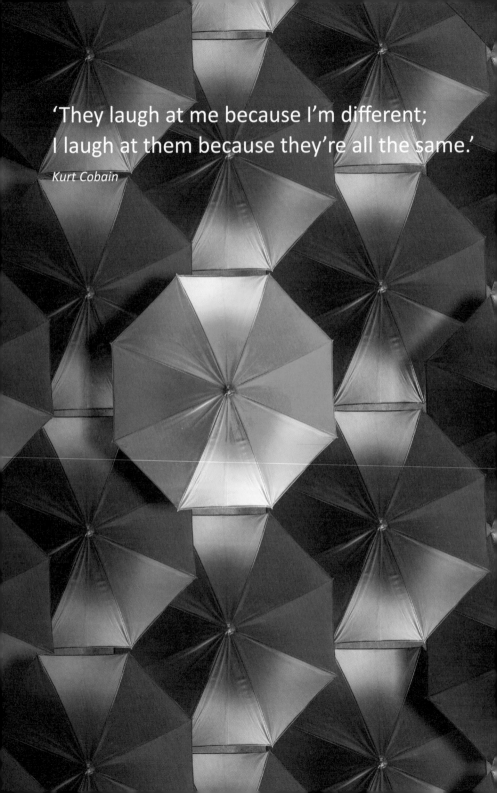

'They laugh at me because I'm different;
I laugh at them because they're all the same.'
Kurt Cobain

THE RINGMASTER

Roll up, roll up. Let the show commence!

This is where we meet your guide -
The Ringmaster - and where we learn
about why this little book exists...

The Ringmaster

As the author of this book I could be called The Ringmaster. So, what entitles me to this exalted position? Am I a doctor? No. A medical professional of any type? No. A teacher? No. Why, then, should you read a book about resilience, growth and wellbeing written by me?

The Serious Bit

Well, my story began around twenty years ago when I lost my first husband. A few years later I lost my mum, then my second husband and, more recently, my eldest son. I don't mean that they died; instead I lost them to depression and stress.

During this time, I wouldn't describe myself as being particularly resilient which is partly why these events were so difficult for me to deal with. But, it's for exactly that reason that I am writing this book!

I learned SO much from personal experience that I want to share everything I know in the hope that this book will equip others with all the knowledge and tools they need to become resilient.

My First Husband

After a wonderful five-year courtship with my first husband we decided to tie the knot. I was ecstatic! The happiness didn't last though and for a number of different reasons we separated just 18 months later.

It was my decision to leave but the guilt was devastating. I became depressed and, over a period of several months, attempted suicide on three separate occasions.

I attribute my ability to rise out of this terrible time not to medication (though that certainly helped me too) but to a wonderful counsellor who treated me with a dose of reality. Perhaps my first experience of resilience in action. She told me that I was not perfect and that to survive this period and to begin to enjoy my life again I had to love and accept myself – warts and all!

I realised that I was feeling sorry for myself and turning myself into a victim, but this behaviour wasn't helping anyone. It was time to take responsibility for my choices, stand up, be accountable and move on. I learned to accept that I am not perfect and I believe that this was the moment I began to love myself unconditionally.

> If the best version of you is less than perfect, that's perfectly OK

My Mum

Losing myself to depression was a painful experience but losing my mum to illness caused by stress took pain to a whole new level.

She was the Assistant Director of Social Work in the area where we lived. A hugely demanding and important job; earned entirely through dedication, hard work and caring.

One day she went to her boss complaining of a sore throat. He sent her to the doctor, and that was the last day she ever worked.

The doctor said she was a 'fixer'; always wanting to make life better for everyone around her, but at this point in time everyone she cared about was having difficulties: at work redundancies were making her staff unhappy, my papa (my dad's dad) was dying, my eldest nephew (only six at the time) had life-threatening cancer, my sister's marriage was falling apart under the strain of the cancer, and my new partner's ex-wife was hauling us through the courts seeking money that we simply didn't have.

All my mum could do was watch as everyone she cared for and loved, suffered. The throat infection was the first physical sign that her mind just couldn't cope and, subsequently, she had a breakdown. Up until this point in my life my mum was my best friend. Anytime I had a problem she was the first person I wanted to talk to.

After her breakdown I didn't just lose my mum, I lost my best friend too. She was still (and always will be) the woman that I love the most in my life, but it was vital to her recovery that at least some areas of her life were happy and in control. So, I stopped sharing my problems with her to help her get better. But no-one could replace her and the loss, at the time was horrendous.

Now, almost twenty years later, my mum is thankfully a lot like her old self and I love her more than ever.

I learned only recently that her recovery was largely down to the absolute dedication of my dad – he is my hero. He made lists of tasks for her every day – she always loved to make lists – and this was the only thing that got her out of bed in the morning. I'm sure my dad didn't know it at the time, but lists are a fantastic resilience tool. It's goal setting in disguise.

My second husband - Tony

Life moved on, Tony and I got married, had a little boy (not in that order!!) and, despite the odd redundancy everything was fine.

Our second son was born almost five years later, and our little family was complete.

Two days after our eldest son's 12th birthday I came home from work to find Tony in a dreadful state lying on the couch. He was grey, shaking and sweating. I know it's a cliché but he honestly looked like death not particularly warmed up.

I think part of it was shock – somehow, he had dodged a well-aimed metaphorical bullet; he had begun to feel a bit strange and then almost blacked out at the wheel whilst driving home from work. Only good fortune (and luckily quiet roads) saved him that day.

After several visits to the hospital and numerous tests nothing conclusive was diagnosed but he was put on to beta blockers (a type of heart medication) and that helped. But we still didn't have an explanation for what was actually wrong. He was having heart palpitations, weird headaches and felt tired a lot of the time. He was scared to drive (not surprisingly) and his personality changed almost completely.

The doctors asked if he might be suffering from stress and we just laughed. Tony never worried about anything and he was a very calm and controlled person. Also, a very strong and capable person. At the time though we didn't actually know what stress is or how it causes illness (neither did the doctors it would seem!!).

Everyone assumes that someone who is stressed runs around like a headless chicken, worrying about everything and, essentially, being a weak person. Wrong, wrong and wrong again!

I have written a whole chapter on stress, so I won't go into it here but, suffice to say, stress is exactly what was causing all of Tony's symptoms. He was eventually diagnosed with SVT (Super Ventricular Tachycardia), a heart condition that will require medication for life – triggered by stress.

For over two years he was a completely different person, a shell of the man he had been before.

This was very hard for me and extremely hard for our sons.

All of this happened around seven years ago. Since then I have become almost an expert on the subject of stress, stress management and resilience – and so has he.

We have learned many lessons; he has fought his way back to health and is now much more like the man I married – but not exactly the same.

This is a good thing though because, through understanding stress and its causes, he has learned to look after himself. He doesn't just assume that he can cope with everything and he doesn't allow others to think that he can either. If he feels tired – he rests, if he needs a break – he takes one, if he doesn't feel 100% he asks me to drive the car; resilience in action!

It's not just Tony who has become resilient – it's both of us – and it's just as well because the biggest challenge of all was just around the corner….

My eldest son

Just over a year after Tony's near black-out he was promoted. This sounds amazing, but it meant we were going to have to relocate from Sussex to the East Midlands. Not such a big deal for Tony and me but, for our children, it was a different matter altogether.

They had spent their whole lives in one town in Sussex and now we were asking them to leave everything they knew and loved behind them to start a new life somewhere they had never been.

If we'd had a choice we would have said 'no' but, as with many things in life, it wasn't that simple. The company that Tony worked for was merging with another and almost everybody was being made redundant. Tony was one of the very few staff that they asked to relocate and, perhaps, the only one who was actually promoted.

At the time our youngest son was just nine years old and we managed to get him into a great school where he made new friends quickly and soon shot to the top(ish) of the class – he's a real bright wee button.

For our eldest son however, all his worst nightmares began to take shape. When he was three years old he was diagnosed with a language disorder. As it happens, this was a mis-diagnosis; he doesn't have a language disorder, he is autistic.

To be fair, this was hard to spot; he was painfully shy (or so we thought) but he was a very lovely boy whose greatest attribute was his kindness. He never hurt anyone physically or emotionally, he worked hard at school even though he found some things very challenging, the teachers all loved him, he was never cheeky, he started doing voluntary work when he was only 12 years old and, and, and, and the list just goes on.

But this is the picture of the perfect child from an adult's perspective. At school everyone thought he was a goody two shoes and so he was bullied again and again.

Before we moved, he still had the friends he had grown up with and so - despite the bullying - he still had a social life of sorts. All of that changed in June 2013.

I had been very careful about selecting what I thought would be the right school. Before leaving Sussex, I had already begun to suspect autism and had started to investigate it with our doctor and the educational psychologist so it was important that any 'new' school understood what was happening and had the right staff in place to deal with it. I honestly thought I had struck gold; I chose a relatively small high school, the SENCO (special needs co-ordinator) seemed very nice and they had links with specialist support for autistic children (if that became the final diagnosis). It all seemed perfect. What's the old adage... if it seems too good to be true then it probably is. I actually don't agree with this but, on this occasion, it couldn't have been more accurate.

The one thing I made clear over and over again to the new school was how shy my son is, and how he would definitely need support to make new friends. This would be the lynchpin to his happiness and success during his main exam years which were approaching rapidly. No problem - they assured me.

Sadly however, they systematically failed to provide support of any kind in this area. He was placed in a tutor group run by the SENCO herself. To be fair she wanted to keep a close eye on him, but her tutor group comprised all of the 'misfits'; the loudest, roughest, toughest most badly behaved kids in the year group – exactly the type of child that my son couldn't understand and simply had no chance of befriending.

Once people found out how 'nice' my son is and how diligent, the bullying started all over again. On top of this he was now beginning to study for his main exams and the pressure was beginning to kick in.

The final blow was a diagnosis of Asperger's Syndrome (a very high functioning form of autism) and this, along with the lack of friends, the bullying and the exams was just too much to for him to bear.

Slowly but surely, he began to fall apart.

For his sake I am not going to discuss all of the details, but I will say that he showed all the classic signs of advancing stress-induced illness: blackouts, panic attacks, severe nightmares, little sleep, withdrawal…. the list goes on and these are only the bits I think he'd be ok with me talking about because these were the bits that others could see anyway. The hidden stuff was SO much worse.

Instead of helping him the school just made things worse. The SENCO tried her best I believe but her hands were tied by the Headmistress (a woman who, in my opinion, should never have been allowed near vulnerable children).

At his lowest point, instead of offering him support, the school excluded him. I should tell you that one of his main goals at school was to never, ever get a detention. He succeeded in this and all his school reports were superb and yet, at his lowest ebb he was excluded. This resulted in us having to take him to the doctor for a suicide assessment.

Six months before the final exams he started having full-blown seizures. The diagnosis for these wasn't epilepsy, it was – as I'm sure you've already guessed – stress.

Thankfully, the seizures didn't happen too frequently and the last one happened just at the beginning of the exams. Then it was almost as if his mind and his body just said, "enough now". He got through the exams without too much trouble and that was the beginning of one of the most remarkable examples of recovery and resilience that I have ever had the privilege to witness.

The great turnaround (and inspiration for this book)

In just two years he completely turned his life around - no longer showing any signs of stress (except nightmares at times when he was under a lot of pressure); he became physically very fit and healthy, choosing to work out any anger or frustration by running and by going to the gym; he got almost the highest marks possible at college and now works full time as a lifeguard; he has a small group of friends; a lovely girlfriend; he's been to Tenerife twice – the first time as a volunteer on a dolphin and whale conservation project and, the second, as a member of staff on the same project. On top of all this – he is now helping other young people who are experiencing similar problems to those he suffered himself.

Recently I suggested everyone in my family create a vision board and his was fantastic. All I told him was that this should be a pictorial representation of his hopes, plans and dreams for the future. By himself, he split it into three sections – short, medium and long term (exactly right for goal setting) and it is inspirational. I am now so excited to watch his life unfold.

My own fate, my own path

One of his short-term goals was to get a tattoo. He fought back on his own and is carving his own path in life. This is what he designed for his tattoo and it's perfect!

Only three years ago I was worried that he would not survive until his 16th birthday. Today I simply can't wait to see what he achieves next. The nicest part of this story is that he's done almost all the work himself. He decided enough was enough, he joined the gym, he knuckled down at college, he set his own goals, he formed friendships and he has smiled more in the last few months than the rest of his life put together. Perhaps he is the one who should be writing this book...

I hope you can see from this little snapshot of my life that I have every reason to understand stress and to want to help others to build resilience. No-one should have to go through the things I have described and yet stress is the number one cause of illness in teenagers and in adults in the UK. That's just wrong.

When my son smiles today it looks like he is glowing from the inside out – it is my goal in life to help as many others as possible to find the light inside that makes them glow and I hope that this book may be a little light switch for you.

This is the vision board that I created when my eldest son did his one. It shows that I want to live by the sea, that family is really important to me, that I love Scotland, that I want to sing, own a Mercedes, have a nice house with a pool, write a book, work all over the world including Australia, help other people to shine and I'd like to have a healthy bank balance.

When life knocks you down, stand up again when you are ready.

Until then, allow others to help you bear the weight.

WHAT IS STRESS?

Being a successful circus performer begins in our head, so this chapter is where we dispel some of the myths around stress and go back to our caveman roots to discover how our natural instincts can help us – or how they can work against us...

Going back to the circus, Big Top performers know that they must train themselves both physically and mentally to achieve success. They must develop a strong mind to be able to push through the physical difficulties that they face as they master their skills.

It's the same in the world outside the circus. We must develop a strong mind to become successful in life. This is called resilience.

Resilience protects us from stress but what is stress, what causes it, and how can it cause physical and/or mental illness? Knowing the answers to these questions will give you a head start in becoming resilient. Knowledge is power!

The first thing that you need to know about stress is that it is NOT an illness. Stress is a chemical reaction in the body that can lead to illness and this can be either physical or mental illness. You cannot be ill with 'stress' but you can have an illness that is caused by stress – this is known as 'stress induced illness'.

Sadly, most people don't understand what stress actually is and there are lots of myths about what kind of people suffer with stress induced illness.

Let's just get that sorted out right now.

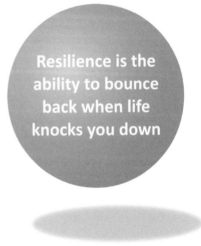

Resilience is the ability to bounce back when life knocks you down

Dispelling the myths

Unfortunately, stress induced illness is often associated with being a weak person. There is a stigma attached to it which means that people are embarrassed to admit they are suffering.

This is very sad because stress induced illness isn't caused by mental weakness. Only people who do not fully understand what stress is think this way. Unfortunately, that seems to be most people – especially in the business world. They are simply under-educated, and it is my hope that books like this one will help them to see things differently.

Stress induced illness most often affects the best people – in school and in business. These are the people who try the hardest, who work the longest hours, who always want to do a good job, who always do their best, who care the most about their results and the people around them. They are life's 'doers' and 'copers' and 'givers'. But, ultimately, you cannot fight nature and nature has a way of forcing us to slow down and look after ourselves.

So, what exactly is stress then?

Well, as I have said already, stress is a chemical reaction in the body. And, to be honest, stress is not always a bad thing. In fact, a bit of pressure (stress) can be very motivating. The problems begin when we are stressed or put under pressure too often.

We can feel stressed by things that happen outside of our body (external) like a difficult or threatening situation, an event or maybe an incident at school, at college, at work or at home. We can also make ourselves feel stressed (internal) simply through our own negative thought patterns or limiting beliefs e.g. "I'm not good enough", "I can't cope," etc. It doesn't really matter whether our stress is external, internal, real or imagined; our brain and body respond in the same way...fight or flight.

What is Fight or Flight?

Fight or flight is a natural human response to threats and it's been this way since we were cavemen.

All those years ago most threats were potentially fatal, for example the sabre-tooth tigers that roamed the lands. Our fight or flight response in this situation was, quite literally, a life-saver. Our bodies would flood with adrenaline and other stress hormones which gave us physical power and courage. Our brains bypassed our thinking skills, bypassed most of our emotions, and focussed entirely on fighting or running away from the threat.

Fast forward to the modern world, and our stress response is exactly the same even though most of today's threats are not potentially fatal: someone yelling at you, too much work – not enough time, sitting an exam, feeling too fat (or too thin), relationship issues, social media pressures (you get the picture).

In the past we needed this stress response to fight the tiger or to run away from it. Today though, that's just not the case. If someone yells

at you it would be unwise to punch them, but you probably wouldn't want to just run away either. Likewise, if you have too much work to do you can't fight this at a physical level and the problem just gets worse if you run away.

So, why does this matter?

Well, let's look a little more closely at what happens to us in fight or flight mode...

The Fight or Flight Response

NOTICEABLE EFFECTS	HIDDEN EFFECTS
Pupils dilate	Brain gets ready for action
Mouth goes dry	Adrenalin released
Neck and shoulder muscles tense	Blood pressure rises
Heart pumps faster	Liver releases glucose for energy
Chest pains, palpitations, sweating	Digestion slows or ceases
Breathing fast and shallow, hyperventilation	Cortisol released to depress the immune system

Our bodies change dramatically. Among other things we begin to breathe faster, systems that our body sees as unnecessary for fight or flight are shut down (like our digestive system – so we lose our appetite), blood is redirected to our muscles, our sight gets sharper, our ability to feel pain lowers and our immune system is suppressed.

Changes also happen in our brain: we lose the ability to think clearly and rationally, we become less able to control our emotions and we cannot readily access our memory banks. No wonder then that we over-react to things and see danger everywhere.

Basically, we are on high alert and we see everything and everyone as a potential threat.

At this point we are in survival mode and positive thinking is almost impossible. Our hearts are closed, and our rational thought is gone.

We make short term choices without thinking about the longer-term impact (perhaps we say things we regret later or lash out when we shouldn't have).

OK, but once the threat has passed, don't we just go back to normal? Well, yes and no.

Fight or flight is a natural response to threats and will happen to everyone from time to time. The real problem arises when this response is triggered too often – for teenagers this could be during an exam period or during sustained bullying. For adults it could be constant pressure at work or a failing marriage – we become increasingly unable to relax and begin to live life in crisis mode, stuck in 'fight or flight'.

As I mentioned earlier, every time the fight or flight response is triggered chemicals are released in to our body. Over time, these accumulate in the body and become toxic.

They start to attack our organs and, in the short to medium term, we begin to suffer one or more of the physical symptoms of stress-induced illness: dizzy spells, blackouts, difficulty concentrating, teeth grinding, eye twitching, diarrhoea, constipation, difficulty sleeping, loss of appetite, sickness, constant colds and infections, panic attacks, headaches, low energy, aches, pains, tense muscles, shaking, seizures...... the list is very long and pretty scary.

Physical symptoms are not the only ones we suffer, there are also emotional symptoms: feeling overwhelmed, agitated, out of control, nervous, moody, low self-esteem, lonely, worthless, depressed, anxious, unable to relax, avoiding others…. an equally long and worrying list.

Left unattended, in the longer term, we can get permanently stuck in fight or flight mode and the hidden effects of this can be a lot more dangerous….

Help, I'm stuck! What happens now?

All of the chemicals flooding our body have begun to attack our organs. We've already discussed the short-term signs and symptoms but over a longer time, more serious things can begin to happen.

The Impact of a Stuck Fight or Flight Response		
PHYSICAL REACTION		LONG TERM IMPACT
Blood pressure rises	→	Heart disease
Stress hormones rise	→	Anxiety, insomnia, addictions, weight gain
Digestive system slows	→	Gastro intestinal problems
Growth and sex hormones fail	→	Premature ageing
Immune system weakens	→	Infections, cancer
Sticky blood platelets increase	→	Heart attacks

For those who believe it is possible to 'snap out' of stress induced illness it may be worth pointing out that the same chemical reactions that cause early symptoms, in the longer term can lead to heart disease or cancer – neither of which you would be expected to cure without a great deal of help and self-care.

The number one cause of illness in teenagers is stress.

For me, the most worrying thing about stress induced illness is that a lot of the time you don't realise you are suffering from it until it's too late. Like my husband, he had no obvious emotional symptoms at all and then, out of the blue, a near black-out whilst driving that could have had fatal consequences.

At this point I want to say two very important things...

1. If you have any of the physical or emotional symptoms listed above – get help, NOW! Go and see your doctor or speak to someone who can help you. Don't ignore it.

2. If you don't have any serious symptoms but are worrying a lot or suspect that you are becoming stressed then read the rest of this book, build up your resilience and learn how to keep your mind and body strong and healthy.

3. If, at any time, you begin to feel out of control or begin to suffer any of the symptoms of stress – get help. Don't assume you can just work through it.

So, now you understand stress, what causes it, and how it can lead to serious illnesses – both physical and mental. Stress induced diagnosable mental health illnesses include:

- Anxiety
- Depression
- Eating Disorders
- Psychosis
- Suicide

It can also trigger other behaviours such as self-harming. But it's not all doom and gloom. It's perfectly possible to learn to cope with challenges and difficulties in life and to remain strong and healthy. We just need to learn (and apply) the skill of resilience.

And so begins our circus training.......

Today's Lessons

- Resilience is the ability to bounce back up when life knocks you down

- Mental and physical illness caused by stress doesn't mean that we are weak in any way. Only people who do not fully understand what stress is think this way

- Stress can be caused by external events or, we can make ourselves feel stressed (internal) through our own negative thought patterns

- Fight or flight is the natural human response to threats. It is our internal alarm system

- In fight or flight mode we lose the ability to think rationally and our body releases chemicals to give us strength to fight or run away from the impending threat

- If we trigger our fight or flight response very regularly, or even get stuck in fight or flight mode, these chemicals build up and start to cause stress induced illness

- Early signs of stress induced illness include headaches, dizzy spells, blackouts, panic attacks, loss of concentration, loss of appetite and lack of ability to sleep

- Longer term physical illnesses caused by stress can include Heart Disease and Cancer

- Stress induced diagnosable mental health illnesses include Anxiety, Depression, Eating Disorders, Psychosis and Suicide

Positive thoughts, positive actions, positive results.

THE BIG TOP MODEL

The 'Big Top' is where all the fun of the circus plays out.

In this chapter you are introduced to your very own 'Big Top' where you can build all the skills you need to become an accomplished circus performer...

Welcome to the Big Top!

Throughout this book we are looking at many different aspects of becoming a skilled circus performer – a strong, resourceful, successful person. To make this possible, we will be learning to juggle three balls at a time – each one representing a key part of life.

Resilience - Growth - Wellbeing

Chapter by chapter we will create a model that can be revised and refined as your skills grow and your focus develops.

And, we will introduce some daily 'bounce-back' practices that will allow you to develop a positive view of your life and of yourself, leading to a strong, inner core of confidence.

The Big Top Model

The model that we will be using is called 'The Big Top Model'. It has lots of different sections in it and we will build it together - step by step. You will end up with a really good picture of who you are, where you're at in life right now and where you would like to get to. It's really simple and it's exciting to watch the picture building.

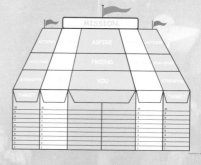

You can download a pdf to print at home as many times as you want for free from the homepage at www.resilientme.co.uk

Everything is achievable
one step at a time

RESILIENCE

Now it's time to burst through the doors of 'The Big Top Model' and rise to the dizzy heights of believing in yourself enough to fly the trapeze. We'll also begin to learn how to juggle, bounce and re-tune.

No time to waste - let's get started...

Juggling Ball Number 1 – Resilience

Resilience is a fancy word but what exactly does it mean?

Well, the Oxford English dictionary describes it as:

- *The capacity to recover quickly from difficulties; toughness*
- *The ability of a substance or object to spring back into shape; elasticity*

Simply put– I think resilience is the ability to bounce back when something knocks you down. And things will knock you down. So, it's not about pretending that there aren't any challenges now, or that there won't be in the future, it's about adapting to them, dealing with them in a constructive way and remaining in control.

It's important to note that resilience does not mean that you will never be sad or angry. These can be necessary emotions to help us deal with our challenges. The important thing is that these negative emotions are just steps along the way and that, in time, we adjust to the challenges and look for ways to learn from them and to 'bounce' back from them.

Some of the things that knock us down though might just surprise you.

Culprit number 1 – yourself!!

Have you ever noticed that some people talk to themselves? Are you one of those people or are you far too sensible for that? Think about it now… are you, or aren't you? Are you, or aren't you? Whoops! There you go talking to yourself…

Actually, the truth is, we all talk to ourselves; pretty much all day, every day. It's how we process the world. Inside our head we have a voice that speaks to us all the time, but this voice can be a positive, supportive one, or it can be a negative, destructive one.

I think of this as life's auto tune so, my questions to you are:

- Which voice do you automatically tune in to?
- What kind of language do you use with yourself?
- Are you your own best friend or, are you your own worst enemy?

Let's have a look at some everyday language we use that might make us feel negative and have a bad effect on our self-confidence...

"I can't do that"

"There's too much to do"

"There isn't enough time"

"I don't enjoy this"

"It's not my fault"

"I can't do anything about it"

"I'm too fat / thin"

"I'm not as pretty / handsome as X"

"Why does this happen to me?"

"I'm not in control of this"

"I'm not as smart / talented as X"

"I can't be bothered"

"I'm too tired"

"I'm waiting for X to sort it out"

"Why am I so stupid?"

Maybe you recognise some of these – maybe you even say some of these to yourself on a regular basis.

When we make these kinds of comments – even as a joke – they chip away at our self-confidence. They make us feel less than we are, and they turn us into a victim. We begin to expect bad things to happen and, guess what? If we expect bad things to happen, they usually do.

I'm going to go off at a little tangent here and tell you about something called the 'Law of Attraction'.

The Law of Attraction

Have you ever noticed that if you walk down the street and smile at a stranger, they smile back? And have you noticed that if you are grumpy or ignore someone that they usually respond in the same way to you?

Our bodies are surrounded by a field of energy and recent medical discoveries have shown that, even when someone loses a leg or an arm, the energy field around where it was still exists and people can still feel real pain even though the limb is gone.

According to the laws of physics positive energy cannot attract negative energy and vice versa.

So, if our energy field is positive – smiling, happy, excited – we automatically attract the same energy from others. If our field is negative then we can only attract negative energy in response.

(BTW - Negative energy has two meanings. One is that the particle is bounded if it has negative energy. This means that positive energy is required to free it from that bound. Another concept of negative energy comes in Relativistic Quantum Mechanics where negative energy is possessed by positrons and positive energy is possessed by electrons. Shivam Choudary, www.quora.com)

Sadly though, for many of us, it is easier to tune in to the negatives rather than the positives and we say things to ourselves that we simply wouldn't consider saying to someone else that we care about.

Getting back to our auto tune…

Using negative language drags us down, makes us feel like we aren't good enough, not up to the task, or being put-upon by others to do all this stuff that we don't want to.

Being resilient is about retuning your thinking to a more positive wavelength. Telling yourself that you are good enough and that all of this effort – even the bits you don't like – is for you. Not for your family, teachers, bosses – not even for your friends. It's all for you so that you can have a happy, successful life; having the freedom, the confidence and the resources to do the things that you want to.

So how do we retune?

I'd say it's a bit like juggling. If you're right-handed you'll be comfortable with throwing and catching a ball in your right hand. But, the first time you try to throw and catch with your left hand, it will feel strange. You might even drop it a few times. It's still the same ball but it feels different now because you are doing something new with it. Add another ball into the mix and it gets more and more tricky – not impossible, but a new skill that you have to learn.

OK, it takes a bit of practise and we don't always get it right, but it is so worth it when we do. What an achievement!

Re-tuning is simply a new skill. It will feel strange at first, and maybe a little difficult, but you'll get used to it and it WILL get easier.

Firstly, what we must never do is pretend the challenge isn't there. So, we would not try to magically change "I can't" into "I can". Instead we take a realistic but positive view of the same situation.

For instance, "I can't" could re-tune to "I can't do that yet". I'm not pretending that I suddenly can but I am setting a positive expectation for the future.

Let's look at another one.... 'There's not enough time'. How could we re-tune this one?

Remember, we have to make this realistic, so you can't just say 'there's loads of time' and expect things to magically change. We need to look at the same problem with positive eyes instead of negative ones so 'there's not enough time' could become something like... 'I will create a schedule and prioritise the tasks'.

Of course, there isn't always a straightforward way to re-tune. Something like 'I don't enjoy this' needs a slightly different thought process. If you genuinely don't enjoy doing something, then that may never change so how could we re-tune?

Well, in this case, you need to consider the bigger picture.... you may not enjoy doing something (like revision or extra work) but how will you benefit from doing it anyway?

Understanding the purpose of it and what you have to gain can provide a more positive attitude towards it. This, then, would re-tune to something like 'what do I have to gain from doing this?'

Now it is time to use your 'Big Top Model' for the first time!

All you need to do is go to the homepage at www.resilientme.co.uk and you can download a pdf to print as many as you want for free.

The door to the big top is the grand entrance to becoming a resilient person. Here is where we will learn to control your inner chatter by looking at your own auto tune and focusing on finding a way to re-tune.

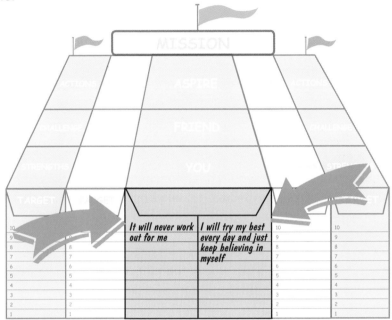

1. I'd like you to think about any negative statements that you say to yourself on a regular basis and write them down on the left hand door.

2. Then, on the right hand door I would like you to re-tune those statements. Look at the same situation and find a positive approach rather than a negative one.

3. Do this now before you progress any further and take as much time as you need. In The Encore - Appendix A I have offered some ideas for re-tuning if you find this exercise difficult.

Listen to the language you use inside your head and, when it is negative, stop yourself and re-tune to a positive version of the same thing.

Culprit number 2 –yourself!! (and bullies)

Another cause of stress is worrying about what other people think of you. This is at its strongest when we are teenagers but it carries on into adult life for many years. Most people don't stop worrying about this until they are well into their forties or fifties.

Worrying is stupid. It's like walking around with an umbrella waiting for it to rain.

But, let's think about it for a moment...If we were all the same the world simply would not function. If we were all doctors, who would be the nurses and who would clean the hospital floors? If we were all carpenters what would happen when someone was sick? Would another carpenter be able to perform surgery or develop drugs to help – I don't think so.

The circus would be a boring place if everyone performed the same act. The thrill is in watching all the different artists perform – experiencing all of the different talents and skills.

And yet it feels SO important to 'fit in', to be the same as everyone else. This is because belonging is a basic human need but, does that mean we should change ourselves to be the same as someone else? Perhaps they should be the ones to change – to become more like us.

> *"Wanting to be someone else is a waste of the person you are"* Kurt Cobain

Each one of us has power in who we are. We all NEED to be different for the world to function, for businesses to function, for schools to function – even for home to function. We can't all be the best athlete, the best boss, the best mathematician, the best artist, the best dancer.... need I go on? Where would the fun in that be? Where would the sense of achievement come from?

Even more importantly, where would our sense of 'self' come from? The things that make us who WE are, that make us interesting? By worrying about what other people think of you, and by seeking approval from someone else, you are handing your power to them. You can no longer make yourself feel good or be proud of yourself because you are allowing someone else's opinion to matter more than yours.

It's important to remember that someone else's opinion is based on their own life experience. Your life experience is different from theirs, so your opinion will be different. It all depends on your perspective.

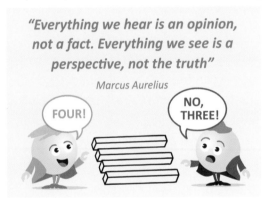

"Everything we hear is an opinion, not a fact. Everything we see is a perspective, not the truth"

Marcus Aurelius

FOUR!

NO, THREE!

We all see the world differently and just because you're not the same as others – even those who appear to be more popular than you - does not mean that you have less to offer the world than they do.

Why would you EVER consider that someone else is more important than you are or, indeed, that you are more important than anyone else? Genuinely nice people don't care if you are the most popular, the fittest, the smartest or the richest; they will like you for who you are. Or they won't.

No matter how hard we try, we can never be liked by everyone. Nor will we like everyone we meet, and that's completely ok. The problem arises when people decide to be deliberately unkind – either through direct confrontation, through undermining you, through physical abuse, through manipulation or through trying to turn others against you. The catch-all phrase for this type of person is a bully.

We often hear about school bullies but, the truth is, there are bullies in all walks of life – at school, at work, in families, sometimes even in friendship groups. In any environment we should not let bullies prevail. We can report them, we can stand up to them and, if necessary, we can avoid them. Only you can be the judge of the best action to take if you encounter a bully.

"Genuinely nice people will like you for who you are. Or they won't. That's completely OK".

The one thing you should never do is try to change yourself to impress them. Why?

Someone becomes a bully because of a weakness in their character or a difficulty in their life. They have a need to control others or to make others feel small so that they can feel powerful. Changing to fit in with their demands simply fuels this need for power and control and ensures that they will continue to treat you – and others – badly. Paying little or no attention to them takes away their power and control.

So, if someone is putting you down, or worse, encouraging others to put you down, just remember that they are coming from a bad place and that they are doing this to cover up their own difficulties. It's hard to see that when it's happening – I know, because I was very badly bullied at school – but you have to trust yourself and own your own power and individuality.

Having said all of that…. to survive in a group, or in a relationship of any kind, we DO have to make compromises. We ARE all different and for different people to exist in harmony with each other they have to adapt to each other. A successful relationship is one where all parties are compromising at a level that they are happy with. Relationships break down when this balance favours one party over the other(s).

Culprit number 3 – yourself!! (and 'helpful' others)

It's not just people putting us down or 'bullying' us that undermines our confidence though. Sometimes it is so much more subtle than that. Sometimes it's actually when people are trying to be nice to you that they can do damage.

Think back to when you were younger. Maybe you were struggling with maths homework or english homework and you asked someone at home to help. They might have helped or they might have been unable to help and so, tried to reassure you by saying something like "Don't worry, I was rubbish at maths too".

But this doesn't reassure. Instead, it plants a seed of doubt in your head that there may be a genetic reason why you are struggling.

And then, every time you find something difficult in maths, it's like pouring water on the seed so it grows stronger and stronger, firmly rooting the belief in your head that you are no good at maths.

Or maybe it wasn't other people, maybe you planted the seeds yourself...

Imagine a scenario in school when you draw a beautiful picture and feel really proud of yourself. Then you look at the drawing of the person sitting next to you and feel that theirs is better than yours, and so the belief that you can't draw is born. Is that true though?

Look at this painting here. In my humble opinion it is just a lot of squiggly lines. Something that any of us could do and yet it's a piece of modern art that sold for $45.5 million!!!

Cy Twombly (1928-2011), Untitled, 2005

"Be careful what you say about yourself because YOU are listening!"

Lisa M Hayes

There will be people in your life who are kind and there will be people who are unkind. And you will be both of these people too – sometimes kind to yourself and sometimes unkind.

Be careful what you say to yourself because you are always listening.

Do not give energy to other people who are unkind and, when you're doing it to yourself, go back to your 'Big Top Model' and re-tune.

Remember: Keep practising this new skill until it becomes second nature

Building the Core

So now we're going to complete the central structure of our Big Top Model and the core of your own resilience.

As you can see from the three confidence crushing culprits above, the one constant is YOU!

- sometimes through negative internal chatter

- sometimes through giving your power away to others (worrying about what they think of you instead of what you think of them)

- sometimes through negatively comparing your skills and talents with those of other people

To become a strong, resilient person we must be our own best friend, we must believe in ourselves and we must value what we have to offer the world. We need to have confidence in ourselves so that when life knocks us down, we can just bounce back up, dust ourselves off and try again.

So, I want you to spend some time now thinking about yourself and all of your best qualities and strengths.

I don't mean your skills. This is not about being good at maths or music; it's about your PERSONAL qualities such as kindness, ambition, diligence, determination, caring, supportive, funny, entertaining and any number of great qualities that you may have.

Make a list of them all and then decide on the three top ones.

List

_____

_____

_____

_____

_____

_____

_____

_____

_____

_____

_____

_____

_____

_____

_____

When you have decided what they are, write them down here in the Big Top model where it says YOU.

NB. During this exercise only POSITIVE statements are allowed!

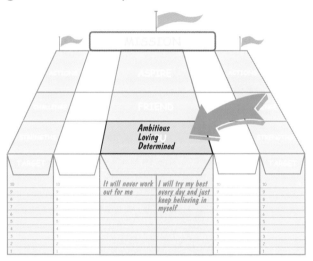

Now I want you to think about the people in your life who love you or really care about you: a family member, a friend or a teacher. What do you think they would say your best qualities are? Again, think of three and write them down where it says FRIEND.

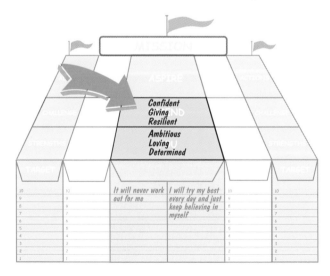

We are beginning to build a positive picture of ourselves from our own perspective and from that of the people who care about us the most. In life, it is important to recognise your own strengths and achievements and to congratulate and reward yourself for them.

To be a resilient individual though, it is also important to have a 'Growth Mindset' (much, much more about this in the next chapter). In other words, it is important to want to grow and continue to develop yourself.

So, to complete this section, I now want you to think of three qualities that you aspire to...

- These may be qualities that you already have but would like to build on

- They may be qualities that you admire in others that you'd like to develop in yourself

- You may have qualities that you dislike (i.e. laziness) so you may decide to change these to more positive qualities such as 'being more engaged' or 'being more active'

Once you have decided, write them down where it says ASPIRE.

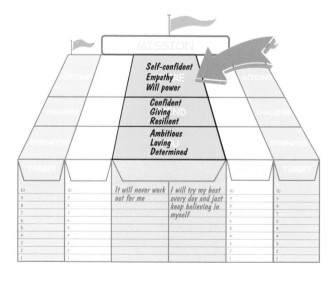

So, being a resilient person is not about pretending that everything is ok and it's not about simply trying to 'tough it out'. It is about choosing to see the positives in any situation by taking the negatives and looking at them in a different way. We're learning to look at difficult things in a positive, constructive way – building ourselves up not beating ourselves up.

Resilience is also about understanding who we are as an individual and what we have to offer – what are our strengths and best qualities? It's ok to be different. We need everyone to be different to make the world function effectively.

Resilience is also about recognising the need to grow, to have something to aim for and to have a purpose in life.

And so our circus training continues...

TODAY'S LESSONS

- Resilience is the ability to bounce back up when life knocks you down

- The three confidence crunching culprits are:

    - Yourself
    - Yourself and bullies
    - Yourself and 'helpful others'

- Control your inner chatter

    - We process the world by talking to ourselves but this voice inside our head can be a positive, supportive one, or it can be a negative, destructive one

    - Listen to the language you use inside your head and, when it is negative, stop yourself and re-tune to a positive version of the same thing

Opinions and perspective

- We need everyone to be different for the world to function successfully

- People's opinions and perspective are based on their experience of life so far and will, inevitably, differ from yours at times

- Worrying about what other people think of you means you are allowing their opinion to be more important than yours; all opinions are equally important

- We all need to feel that we 'belong' but a healthy, successful relationship is one where all parties are compromising at a level that they are happy with

- Do not give in to bullies; Paying little or no attention to them diminishes and, eventually, takes away their power and control

Unhelpful comparisons

- Sometimes, when people are trying to make us feel better they can accidentally make us doubt our own abilities

- Everyone has different skills and talents; you only ever have to be the best version of you

- To become a strong, resilient person we must be our own best friend, we must believe in ourselves and we must value what we have to offer the world

- Understand WHO you are, what your personal strengths and qualities are, what people who care about you think, and how you would like to grow as an individual

- Build yourself up; don't beat yourself up!!

Find your inner sparkle.

GROWTH

Now we are ready to take your juggling skills to the next level and we're going to add in a few more circus skills - mastering the balance board first, then stepping up onto the tightrope where we must keep our focus firmly on the way ahead.

In here you will also learn how to eat an elephant, how to become a human satnav and you can use the trapeze to fly as high as you like.

Lots to do, no time to waste, let's go!

Juggling Ball Number 2 – Growth

Recognising the need to grow, to have something to aim for, to have a purpose in life is known as having a **growth mindset.**

The desire to grow is an important factor in being resilient, so ball number 2 is all about Growth.

At many times in our life we are told how clever we are or how talented. At school we are often streamed into sets. This is to ensure that you are taught at a level and at a pace that your school believes you can cope with. Unfortunately though, this can also lead to us having limiting beliefs about what we are truly capable of achieving.

As you know, my son was mis-diagnosed with a language disorder when he was three years old. For the entire duration of his school education he was treated as a child with 'learning difficulties', always placed in the lower or middle sets and automatically entered for lower papers in maths and english.

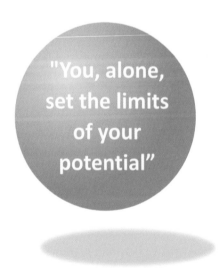

"You, alone, set the limits of your potential"

Even when the maths tutor we paid for stopped tutoring him because he was too good (he taught him physics instead) the school still refused to move him on to the higher paper.

He passed his exams but only at the lower levels – unlike his college results!

When he went to college he was no longer 'pigeon-holed'. The college started everyone at the same level and allowed them to develop according to their desire to work and succeed – not their assumed ability.

Not surprisingly, with the absence of limiting beliefs, he left college with outstanding results.

Ability, intelligence and talent are not pre-determined. Everyone is born with natural levels of intelligence and talent, but this is just the starting point. What actually determines the end-point is your own levels of self-belief and determination. If you want to succeed, you will. You just have to be prepared to work hard and to be determined no matter how difficult the pathway is.

Ability is only 10% of capability; the other 90% is up to you. How determined are you? How badly do you want to succeed?

The Human SatNav

I keep talking about success, but what does it actually mean? Truthfully, it means very different things to different people; money, possessions, position, power, popularity, fame, supporting others, charitable work, happy family, happy children, talent, academic achievement, the list goes on and on.

THE PATH TO SUCCESS

What people think it looks like   What it actually looks like

It doesn't matter what type of success you desire, there is one, indisputable fact - success is not a straight road from A to B – success is knowing where you want to be, knowing what you want to achieve, setting these targets clearly in your head and keeping your eye on them no matter what difficulties life throws at you.

Anyone that you respect or admire in life has kept their eye on where they want to be and has followed a road of many ups and downs to get there – just like a human satnav.

Think about it...

When you enter a postcode into a satnav you are identifying your destination – where you want to get to.

The satnav will select and follow the easiest, most direct route. When you encounter some roadworks the satnav simply says 'recalculating' and it works out another route before heading towards its destination once again.

Later, you may encounter a road accident. This time you may have to go back a few miles before you can move forward again. The satnav will simply say 'recalculating' and find yet another way of reaching its destination. No matter how many detours it has to take, a satnav will always get to its destination – eventually. I have NEVER heard a satnav say "look, just give up and go home!"

To achieve our goals, to succeed, we simply need to become a human satnav. There are many fantastic examples of famous people who have succeeded against the odds – perfect examples of human satnavs in action...

Walt Disney was fired from his job as a newspaper reporter because his boss said he "lacked imagination and had no original ideas".

Lionel Messi was cut from his football team because a growth hormone deficiency made him smaller than the other boys.

Oprah Winfrey (the MOST powerful woman in television) was fired from her job as a news anchor and her boss told her she "was not fit for television".

Abraham Lincoln (the 16th President of America) was beaten in eight elections, his fiancée died and he had a nervous breakdown but he simply never gave up his dream of becoming President.

These people all had one thing in common – the desire to succeed and the determination to keep on trying until they did. It wasn't easy for any of them, they didn't have special contacts, privileges or money – they were just prepared to keep chasing their dreams no matter how many difficulties they had to deal with along the way.

Setting Goals

Clearly, these people knew exactly what they wanted. They had set goals and were aiming to achieve them. But what exactly is a goal and how do we set them?

For many of us, a goal is what footballers score in a match (hopefully). The goal posts give them something to aim for, a way of measuring their progress and a way of 'winning' the match, the cup, the league...without the goals to aim for, what would be the point of the match?

This is exactly the same in life. If we can see what we are aiming for then we can measure our progress and we'll know when we have 'won'. We will also be able to deal with difficulties along the way as long as our main focus stays clearly set on our goals.

 Goals can be short, medium or long term and the best idea is to have a mixture of all of these. However, it is also vitally important that we set the goals that will ensure progress across all of the different areas of our lives.

All too often people put the pursuit of money, fame, sporting or business success ahead of everything else and then wonder why their lives are unhappy even when they have reached their goal.

You only have to look at the sad examples of celebrities who turn to drugs or alcohol or even take their own lives to know that success in just one area doesn't necessarily lead to happiness and contentment.

The key to achieving happiness, contentment and success is to set a balance of goals across all of the areas in your life.

Balance

There are many different areas in our lives that are important and we are at our happiest when all areas are balanced.

This picture shows a piece of circus equipment called a rolla bolla. Circus performers do all kinds of amazing balancing tricks on them, but the main skill involved is making constant adjustments.

Every time the board wobbles they adjust – and this is the same in life. We will just find some sense of balance and then something will change and we need to adjust to deal with that change.

"Nothing is certain except change"
Anon

In fact, change is about the only thing in life that is certain so we really need to learn how to deal with it effectively. The first thing to do is have a good, honest look at the balance in our lives right now – take a snapshot, if you like. This way we can see where our current strengths are and we can identify where our weaknesses are. This gives us a starting point then for our road to success.

You might have heard people talking about the work / life balance, but it doesn't just refer to adults – it refers to you too.

On one side of our rolla bolla we have our work demands – things like school, homework, studying, revision. On the other we have our life needs, things like health, fitness, hobbies, relaxation, friendships.

Using the Big Top Model we are going to look at four categories within your work / life balance.

The first category is **Attendance & Attitude.**

What do I mean by this… well, it's things like…

- Being at school/college on time every day
- Wearing the right uniform in the right way
- Bringing all of the right equipment to school
- Listening in class (ALWAYS!)
- Joining in with everything and making the most of all opportunities
- Giving 100% effort (ALWAYS!)

So, what we're going to do is label section 1 at the bottom of the Big Top Model – Attendance and Attitude.

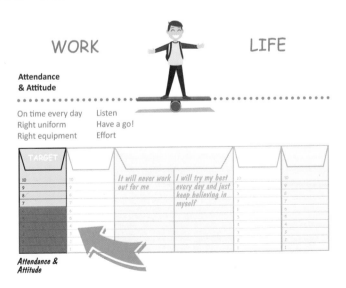

You can see that this section has numbers from 1 to 10. Be completely honest and give yourself a score. One is absolutely awful, 10 is perfect. Draw a line at the right point in the first section and colour it in.

The next category is Independent Learning. This category is all about expanding our knowledge outside of the classroom. Sometimes it will be tasks that your teachers will have set but, often it is about you voluntarily seeking to build your knowledge base. For this section we follow the same process. So, now we're looking at things like...

Homework – do you always do your homework on time, do you do it to the very best of your ability and is it always beautifully presented? Or, do you do the minimum that you can get away with, in a rush, looking awful?

Studying – do you take time to learn as much as you can about your subjects, looking back at your notes and trying to expand your knowledge?

Reading Around – do you actively look for other books or websites on the subjects you are studying and read as much as you can - independently of what the teacher has asked you to do?

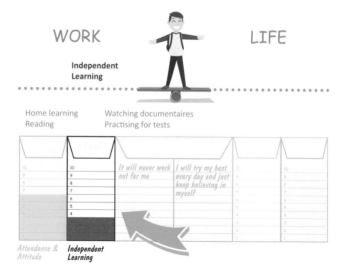

Do you revise regularly – not just when a test or exam is coming up?

Do you watch documentaries and videos on YouTube to expand your knowledge?

Once again, assess your Independent Learning honestly and give yourself a score from 1 to 10 then colour it in.

Now we're moving over to the 'Life' side of our Rolla Bolla and our first category is Health & Fitness.

Exercise – do you exercise regularly? It doesn't matter what kind of exercise it is, as long as it makes you slightly breathless. For ongoing mental and physical good health regular exercise means 20 minutes, 5 times a week.

Diet – Do you have a balanced diet? A mixture of healthy fruit and vegetables as well as fun (naughty) stuff like chocolate and cakes? Do you drink enough fluid? We need 2 litres a day and the best way to get this is by drinking water.

Anything containing sugar (fizzy drinks and more than one fruit juice a day), caffeine (tea, coffee, energy drinks, coca-cola and a number of other fizzy drinks) or alcohol doesn't count towards this.

Relaxation – This includes things like reading, playing sports, meditating, walking, etc. It does NOT include watching television or being in front of any type of screen that uses light on the blue wavelength, including computers and smart phones.

Sleep – science has proven that for healthy brain development in teenagers you need to get between 8 & 10 hours sleep every night. I will look at sleep in more detail later and explain why you need this but, for the purposes of giving yourself a score in this section, you must stick to the amounts given here.

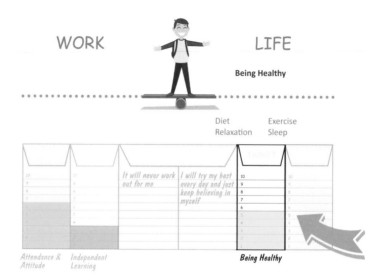

WORK   LIFE

Being Healthy

Diet   Exercise
Relaxation   Sleep

			It will never work out for me	I will try my best every day and just keep believing in myself		
10					10	10
9					9	9
8					8	8
7					7	7
					6	
		4				
Attendance & Attitude	*Independent Learning*				**Being Healthy**	

So, as before, label the Health & Fitness section and then give yourself an honest score. The more honest we are at this stage, the more realistic the picture of our life balance is at this point in time.

Our final section in the work / life balance is Extra-Curricular activities – the 'fun stuff' if you like!

So, how much time do you spend with your friends? This must be in person, not over the internet courtesy of a head set or X-Box live!

Do you have any hobbies? Ideally, we would want to have more than one as variety makes life fun and interesting. Reluctantly I will allow computer games to be a part of this.

Are you a member of any clubs? Being part of a group or a team is hugely beneficial for our feelings of self-worth and belonging – one of the most basic needs that a human being has.

Do you like to try new things and have new experiences? This could be sports, holidays, different foods, books that you wouldn't normally read, computer games you wouldn't normally play, CCF, Duke of Edinburgh, etc.

Once again, label the section and give yourself a score. Don't forget to colour it in.

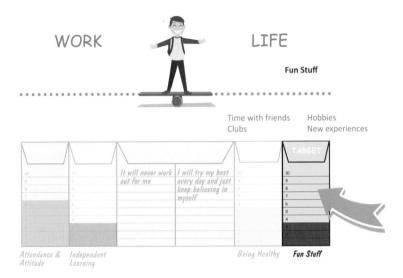

Well done! You now have an accurate picture of the balance in your life right now. Take a moment to think about it and notice where your strengths and your weaknesses are.

Now, if you look at my Rolla Bolla, you will see that....

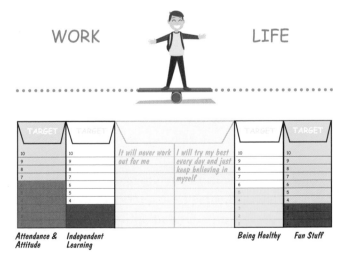

I scored a 6 for Attendance & Attitude – this was my highest score – and I scored a 3 for Independent Learning and Extra-Curricular activities. These were my lowest scores.

So, I am good at my job, but I don't have much variety in my life and I am not focussing enough on developing myself outside of my job. What we want to aim for is a balance in all areas.

In the happiest world for you every part of your life would be at roughly the same level.

Decision Time

Now we have established what our work/life balance looks like, it is easy to see where the highs and lows are, our areas of strength and weakness.

Armed with this information, we are ready to set some goals to create the perfect work/life balance.

Setting goals isn't just a simple case of randomly picking something and hoping that you will achieve it one day. It is a process that has to be approached with serious intent and, one stage at a time.

Many people write whole books on goal setting but I am going to keep it very simple here and introduce you to a system that works within the 'Big Top Model'.

"If it's important to you, you will find a way"

(I would recommend a fantastic book written by a friend of mine – Goal Mapping by Brian Mayne). When I am setting goals, I like to use the word target as it makes me feel as if I am aiming for something, but a target is nothing more than a weak wish inside our head until we have given it a deadline.

So, step number 1 is to decide when we wish to hit our target.

Step 1. Decide on your target date and write it on the Big Top Model

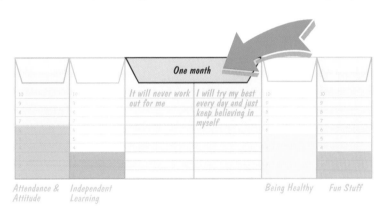

When you set a target don't make the mistake of taking on too much at once. Targets should always be challenging but achievable. The challenge motivates us, and the achievement allows us to feel that we are making constant progress.

If our target is too big, there is a real danger that we will simply give up when things get difficult. After all, if you decide to run a marathon, you don't go out and run 26 miles straight away; you set yourself smaller training targets and this is the same thing.

We are going to set a target for each section in the work/life balance. Most of your efforts should go into improving your weakest area so this will be your most challenging target.

At the time of writing, for me this was about improving the number of extra-curricular activities in my life, so I decided to set a target to start a new hobby and that this hobby would be singing.

Step 2. Decide what you would like your main target to be and write it on the Big Top Model

When you set a target, you MUST always write it down as if it is something you have already achieved. This gives the brain a very clear picture of what you want to achieve.

Avoid saying things like... "I want to learn to sing". Instead say... "I am learning to sing", or even " I can sing".

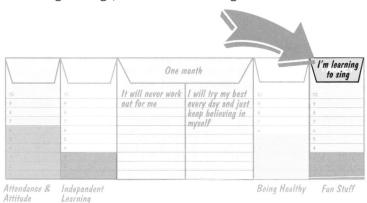

		One month			I'm learning to sing
10	10	It will never work out for me	I will try my best every day and just keep believing in myself	10	10
9	9			9	9
8	8			8	8
7	7			7	7
6	6			6	6
5	5				5
4	4				4

Attendance & Attitude   Independent Learning   Being Healthy   Fun Stuff

Remember 'balance' is what matters – not that every area is a ten straight away. You can work towards this as you move through school and through life and, as life changes, you will need to make constant adjustments.

"All you have to be is the best version of you"

Now you should set small, much easier targets for the remaining three areas. This is just to ensure that we are always paying attention to each area of our life and that we are always growing.

Step 3. Decide what you would like your smaller targets to be and write them on the Big Top Model

Set targets to raise your game one step at a time. You simply revise your targets as your balance improves.

I wrote a chapter	Read two books	One month		Meditate each day	I'm learning to sing
10	10	It will never work out for me	I will try my best every day and just keep believing in myself	10	10
9	9			9	9
8	8			8	8
7	7			7	7
	6			6	6
	5			5	5
	4			4	4
				3	3
				2	2
				1	1

| Attendance & Attitude | Independent Learning | | | Being Healthy | Fun Stuff |

Just a note...

At this point, I would like to say that sometimes we do have to go out of balance deliberately if something important is happening, like exams for example. During an exam period you may spend more time on the work side of your life but, provided it's not too extreme and doesn't last for an extended period of time, this is ok.

This doesn't mean that you can ignore the other areas of life, rather that you may have to spend a little less time with friends or reduce the amount of time you spend on hobbies, but you must make sure that you still allow time for looking after your health and fitness and making sure you get enough relaxation and sleep.

Once this 'difficult' period is finished you must immediately re-adjust the balance in your life to feel happy and in control.

Be Your Own Life Coach

A life coach is someone who helps you to set and achieve your goals. They support and motivate you when things get difficult and they help you to stay on track so that you can reach your full potential. A good life coach is a very valuable asset but, as is often the case, people who are good at what they do are expensive.

However, it IS possible to coach yourself by following a few simple steps. And, if things get tough, you can partner up with a friend and help each other to achieve your goals.

So, now that we've set our targets, we are going to coach ourselves through the process of achieving them.

Everybody has different strengths and weaknesses and you need to understand yours to make positive progress in life.

For each target you have set you will already be good at some things that will help you to achieve it – this is a strength.

For my main target I know that I really enjoy singing so this is definitely a strength. I also have various different strengths that will help with my other targets. Of course, sometimes the same strength can help you to achieve lots of different targets.

Create your vision, commit to it and watch it flourish.

Step 4. On the Big Top Model, write down the strengths you already have that will help you to achieve each of your targets

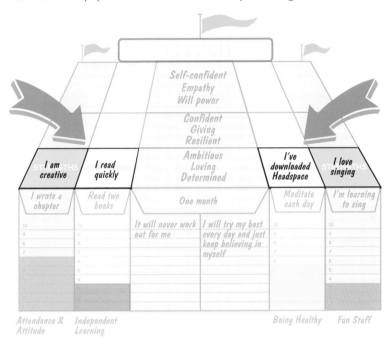

		Self-confident Empathy Will power			
		Confident Giving Resilient			
I am creative	I read quickly	Ambitious Loving Determined		I've downloaded Headspace	I love singing
I wrote a chapter	Read two books	One month		Meditate each day	I'm learning to sing
10 9 8 7	10 7 6 5 4	It will never work out for me	I will try my best every day and just keep believing in myself	10 9 8 7 6	10 9 8 7 6 5 4
Attendance & Attitude	Independent Learning			Being Healthy	Fun Stuff

Now, each target will also present you with some challenges – I guess you could call these weaknesses. If we had no weaknesses, then we would always be in perfect balance.

Everybody has weaknesses and it is actually a strength to understand ourselves well enough to identify them. This is the first stage of overcoming them and gives us a great sense of progress and achievement.

Rocognising your weaknesses is a strength

Step 5. On the Big Top Model, write down the challenges that you will need to overcome so that you can achieve each of your targets

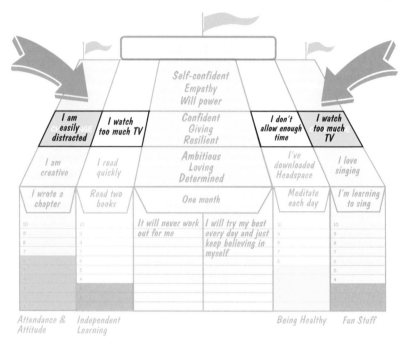

Once we have identified our strengths and weaknesses, we can then consider the actions we need to take to achieve our targets.

Remember, we must work towards our targets one step at a time, and so it is likely that there will be several actions that you need to take, and you may need to keep adding to this part of the Big Top Model. We don't always know every action that will be necessary so just start with the first one or two and move on from there.

So, you should think about this exercise very carefully and identify the first one or two steps needed to start working towards your targets. Remember, you have a whole month to achieve them, so you don't need to do everything at once. You just need to have a clear plan and that is exactly what the Big Top Model is.

Can you eat an elephant?

A teacher once asked me if it is possible to eat an elephant. I thought about it carefully and then said "yes, if you cut it up into little pieces".

The teacher frowned at me and said "what do you have to do before you cut it up?"

I smiled and said, "kill it".

"Yes, but what do you have to do before you kill it?" she said.

"Oh, I see where you're going with this" I said. "First you would have to find it, then you would have to catch it, THEN you would kill it, chop it up into little pieces, cook them and eat them one at a time".

I realised that the elephant was an analogy for a large target. You cannot achieve it all at once. Rather, you must identify the very first step and then work in bite-size chunks, one step at a time until you have achieved success.

Step 6. On the Big Top Model, write down the first actions you will need to take to achieve each of your targets

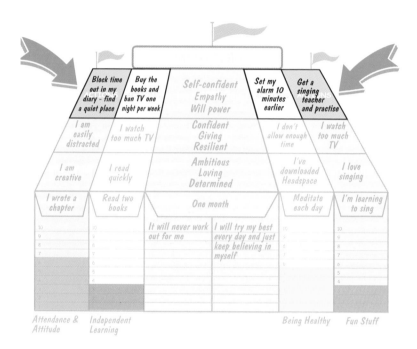

Block time out in my diary - find a quiet place	Buy the books and ban TV one night per week	Self-confident Empathy Will power	Set my alarm 10 minutes earlier	Get a singing teacher and practise	
I am easily distracted	I watch too much TV	Confident Giving Resilient	I don't allow enough time	I watch too much TV	
I am creative	I read quickly	Ambitious Loving Determined	I've downloaded Headspace	I love singing	
I wrote a chapter	Read two books	One month	Meditate each day	I'm learning to sing	
10 9 8 7	10 9 8 7 6 5 4	It will never work out for me	I will try my best every day and just keep believing in myself	10 9 8 7 6 5	10 9 8 7 6 5 4
Attendance & Attitude	Independent Learning			Being Healthy	Fun Stuff

Now I'm on a Mission….

You almost have a complete Big Top Model for Resilience now but there is one very important decision left to make.

Why are you bothering to do this? What is the point of all this effort and self-improvement?

I would call this your BIG reason why – or – your mission!

When someone has a mission, they are full of commitment and passion. When we know why we are working towards something it helps us to deal with whatever bumps we hit along the way.

So, what is your big reason why, what is your mission?

It can be anything, small or large. It can be short term or long term and it can be about almost anything – in school, at home or in life.

Some examples might be…

- To get the best exam results possible
- To feel really good about myself
- To always be the best version of me
- To make a lot of money
- To get a great job
- To go down in history
- To travel the world
- To respect myself and others
- To always be there for my family
- To be a strong, resilient person
- To embrace change and growth

He who has a reason why, can bear almost any how
Friedrich Nietzsche

Step 7. Think carefully about why it will benefit your life to achieve these targets and then write down your mission on the Big Top Model

Big Top Model diagram:

Top banner: **To be the happiest, healthiest and smartest version of myself**

Attendance & Attitude	Independent Learning			Being Healthy	Fun Stuff
Block time out in my diary - find a quiet place	Buy the books and ban TV one night per week	**Self-confident Empathy Will power**		Set my alarm 10 minutes earlier	Get a singing teacher and practise
I am easily distracted	I watch too much TV	**Confident Giving Resilient**		I don't allow enough time	I watch too much TV
I am creative	I read quickly	**Ambitious Loving Determined**		I've downloaded Headspace	I love singing
I wrote a chapter	Read two books	One month		Meditate each day	I'm learning to sing

Goal-setting columns:

Attendance & Attitude	Independent Learning			Being Healthy	Fun Stuff
10	10	It will never work out for me	I will try my best every day and just keep believing in myself	10	10
9	9			9	9
8	8			8	8
7	7			7	7
	6			6	6
	5			5	5
	4			4	4
				3	
				2	2
				1	1

Congratulations!!! You have now completed the Big Top Model and are ready to graduate from circus school...... or are you?

There is one more aspect of circus life to consider. Circus performers do not stay fit and healthy by practising every now and again. They may review their act every month, or every quarter, just as you will review your Big Top Model periodically; but, to stay fit and healthy they must train every day.

And so our circus training continues....

Life may determine who you are in the beginning; it's YOU who determines who you are in the end.

TODAY'S LESSONS

- The desire to grow is an important factor in being resilient;
  "To grow is to live" Rachel Munns

- Ability is only 10% of capability; the other 90% is up to you

- Success is not a straight line from A to B – success is knowing
  where you want to be, knowing what you want to achieve,
  setting clear targets and working towards them no matter what

- Setting targets gives you something to aim for but you must
  follow some simple rules to complete this task effectively
    - Always set a deadline for your target
    - Targets should be challenging but achievable
    - Balance in life creates happiness so create a target for each
      aspect of your life
    - Targets must be positive and written in the present tense –
      as if you have already achieved them

- Become your own life coach
    - Identify the strengths you have that will help you to achieve
      your targets
    - Identify any challenges (weaknesses) you have
    - Set actions to work towards your target – taking one
      manageable step at a time
    - Ask your friends to help you stay motivated when things are
      tough

- He who has a reason why can bear almost any how
    - Identify the BIG reason why you want to reach your targets

Focus on what's good;
fix what isn't.

FIRE EATING, KNIFE THROWING AND TAKING RISKS

The circus is full of excitement and danger
- just like life really. In this chapter we learn
the delights of taking a little risk or two....

Fire-Eating, Knife Throwing and Taking Risks

In the last chapter I asked you if you like to try new things and have new experiences?

Most people would say 'yes' to this question but is that really the truth? How many times do you think a UK citizen will try something new before giving up?

The answer is less than one. Tragic.

Most people avoid trying new things just in case it doesn't go perfectly or, perhaps, because it might be a little embarrassing. It feels like too much of a risk!

> ## What do you see?
> # OPPORTUNITYISNOWHERE
> Whether you see it or not, opportunity is now here...always.

SO many people miss out on SO many opportunities because of the fear of failure and yet, no-one ever achieved success without making many, many mistakes along the way.

This, sadly, is almost epidemic amongst teenagers – always trying to impress, always trying to fit in, terrified of looking silly.

BUT how will you ever know what you could be amazing at if you don't grab hold of every opportunity that you are offered and, if you don't go out and seek as many opportunities as possible?

Let me tell you a little story...

Thomas Edison was one of the 20th century's greatest inventors and a highly regarded scientist. His quest to invent the electric lightbulb attracted a lot of interest.

After he had 'failed' to find a solution 5000 times there was a press conference. At this conference a young reporter stood up and challenged Thomas.

"Mr Edison, don't you think it's about time that you stopped wasting the government's money on this nonsense that you call the electric lightbulb? You have failed 5000 times!"

Now, whilst most people would have felt embarrassed by this type of public assault, Thomas simply stood and gave his response – one that demonstrated absolute self-belief.

"My dear boy, I have not 'failed' 5000 times. I have successfully identified 5000 ways that don't work".

It took him almost 10,000 attempts but never once did he believe he was failing. He simply believed that every 'failure' was a learning opportunity and a step closer to success.

What do we learn from this story?

If Thomas had allowed fear of failure or possible embarrassment to get in his way, we may never have had the electric light bulb as we know it.

The only time in life that we actually fail is when we simply give up.

Today's Lesson

Fear of failure means that most people give up
on things without even trying.

The only time we actually fail is when we don't
try or when we give up!

OUR BEAUTIFUL BRAIN

Circus performers must train their mind as well as their body.

Here we delve into the depths of our brain and learn how to use drugs safely, to power all the mobile phones in the world and how balloons can save the day!

Our Beautiful Brain

So far, we have learned to juggle two balls – resilience and growth. We know that we need to develop positive self-talk and a positive self-image to feel good about ourselves. We also recognise the need to grow in a balanced and focussed way underpinned by setting clear targets and coaching ourselves through the process of working towards them.

These are all necessary and very healthy habits to develop and, over time, they will lead us to develop a resilient mind which will help us to deal with the worries, pressures and stresses in our life in a calm and constructive manner.

In an ideal world we will develop our skills to the point where we can significantly reduce the number of times we trigger our fight or flight response, but to do this we need to better understand our brain.

So, we are going to take a little break from our circus training to find out more......

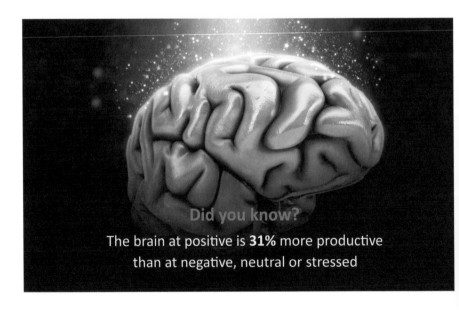

Did you know?

The brain at positive is **31%** more productive than at negative, neutral or stressed

Fight or Flight – the Brain

Earlier in this book we examined what stress is, how our natural stress response puts us into fight or flight mode and the effect that this has on our body.

What we didn't look at is what happens to the brain when this natural response is triggered.

The brain has three different levels:

- the reptilian brain - where the emotional centre the amygdala resides

- the mammalian brain - where our memory banks are

- the pre-frontal cortex – this is the part of our brain that separates us from the animal kingdom because this is where rational thought lives; our ability to think things through and to reason.

All parts of the brain are kept alive by the blood that pumps around it. Contained within the blood supply is oxygen which the brain needs to function. However, when we go into fight or flight mode the brain redistributes this oxygen channelling most of it into the amygdala.

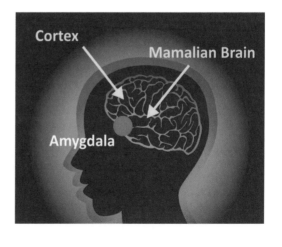

This has the effect of slowing down our access to the mammalian brain which reduces the control we have over our emotions and also makes it harder to remember things. In an exam, for example, fight or flight mode could lead to mental blocks.

It also reduces the capacity of our pre-frontal cortex so we lose the ability to think rationally. This is why people behave in ways they wouldn't normally when they are angry, upset and so on.

In today's world there are many, many pressures that can cause a teenager to go into fight or flight mode:

- Any strong negative emotion such as anger, fear, upset, worry, nerves

- Anything that is – or appears to be – threatening

- Relationship issues with friends, with family, with teachers or with colleagues if you have a job

- Social Media – when it is used as a tool for bullying or when you feel your life doesn't match up to other peoples'

- Revision and exam pressure

- Peer pressure - trying to fit in, be cool, keep up

- Hormones

- Appearance – too tall, too short, too thin, too fat, too many spots, imperfect hair, the 'wrong' clothing or brand names

And so the list goes on.

Some of these pressures build up over time and you need to apply the lessons you have already learned to build up your resilience.

However, sometimes a single event can put you straight into fight or flight mode – like an argument, an audition, an interview, an exam, a nasty social media post and even your own negative thoughts which we will look at more closely in a moment.

When this happens we know that the body floods with chemicals and we know that parts of the brain slow down, BUT did you know that you can regain control of your brain almost instantly?

We can calm ourselves down, get rid of nerves, overcome fears just by learning a simple breathing technique.

There are many different deep breathing techniques but the one that I am going to describe to you is called balloon breathing.

To begin, you must either stand up straight or sit up straight so that your lungs are not being restricted in any way. You then breathe in through your nose for a count of around 5 seconds. As you breathe in, imagine that you are inflating a balloon in your tummy – so your tummy actually grows bigger just like a balloon would. This allows as much oxygen as possible to enter your lungs.

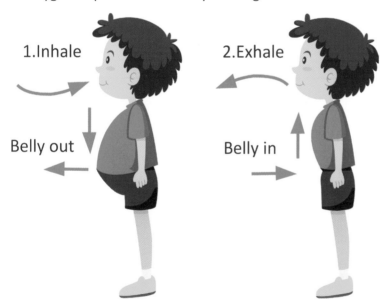

1.Inhale

Belly out

2.Exhale

Belly in

Breathe out through your mouth for a count of 7. At the same time, deflate the balloon, using your tummy muscles to push the air (now carbon dioxide) out of your body.

Repeat this a number of times for a minute or two.

This will re-oxygenate the brain allowing you to calm down and to think more clearly.

Sometimes, particularly if you suffer badly from anxiety, you might also want or need to remove yourself from the situation temporarily until you feel in control again.

This could be by going to a 'safe' place in the school, college, home, etc. or maybe even going outside for a short walk (if the circumstances allow you to do this).

Be careful though, deep breathing re-oxygenates the brain but it does not stop the flow of chemicals into your body so we still need to continue our circus training to protect ourselves from the potentially harmful effects of this process.

But first, a little more about the brain.

The Power of Positive Thinking

Inside our head we have an average of 100 billion brain cells.

When we are thinking, learning, feeling, in fact doing anything at all, our brain cells have to communicate with each other and they do this by using electricity.

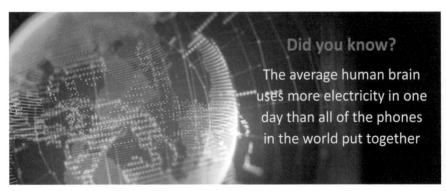

Did you know?

The average human brain uses more electricity in one day than all of the phones in the world put together

The electrical signal starts in the nucleus of the brain cell (picture A). It then travels along the dendrite and crosses over the gap in between known as the synaptic gap thus linking two brain cells together. Just one thought can link many thousands of brain cells together.

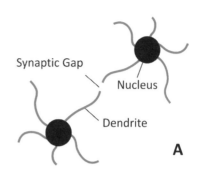

A

Picture B shows what it actually looks like inside our brain when brain cells are communicating with each other.

If we are feeling happy, excited, interested or positive in any way, our brain releases a natural chemical called Serotonin. The nickname for Serotonin is 'the happy drug'.

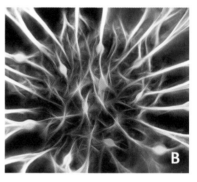

B

It quite literally makes our brain happy and when this happens the electrical signals speed up so that our brain works more effectively

However, if we are feeling unhappy, bored, stressed, disinterested, or any negative emotion, the brain releases a chemical called Cortisol instead (you may remember this chemical from our chapter on stress).

Cortisol does the opposite of Serotonin. It slows our brain processes down so that we find it difficult to think clearly, difficult to learn and, ultimately, difficult to cope.

So, positive thinking actually alters the chemicals in our brain and increases our chances of doing well in life.

Now that we understand more about how our brain works, we are ready to complete our circus training....

- When the brain is positive it is 31% more productive than at neutral, negative or stressed

- The brain has three different levels:
    - *reptilian* - amygdala
    - *mammalian* - memory and emotional centre
    - *pre-frontal cortex* – thought and reason

- In fight or flight mode oxygen in the brain is redistributed and reduces our ability to think clearly, to control our emotions and to access our memory

- We can take the brain out of fight or flight mode through deep breathing exercises

- The average human being has 100 billion brain cells that communicate with each other through electrical signals
    - each brain uses more electricity in one day than all of the world's phones put together

- When we are feeling positive we release a chemical called Serotonin which increases the speed of our brain allowing us to perform better

- When we are feeling negative we release a chemical called Cortisol which slows down our brain making it harder to think, learn and cope

- Positive thinking actually increases our chances of doing well in life

When you stop doing things the way you've always done them...

...you'll start seeing things the way you've never seen them.

Your thoughts are
a magnet.

Worry attracts
difficulty, hope attracts
possibility, and belief
attracts confidence
and action.

Positivity is a choice.

WELLBEING

This is where we finally master our juggling skills, we learn weird things about sleep and we see that goals give us control.

We learn how to walk on fire, that we can be programmed just like a computer and that we must fit our own mask first.

Let's continue our training....

Juggling Ball Number 3 – Wellbeing

To become a fully-fledged circus performer, we now need to learn to juggle ball number 3 which is looking after our wellbeing – not periodically, but on a daily basis.

To do this effectively we need to take a holistic approach towards wellbeing that looks after our body, our mind and our spirit.

The Body

Looking after our body is simple but it is not always easy as it requires a certain amount of self-discipline.

Firstly, we need to do some cardio exercise five times a week for twenty minutes at a time. It doesn't have to be high energy, but it does need to raise our heartbeat and make us slightly out of breath. There's no need to go to the gym (unless you particularly want to), you can simply go for a brisk walk or a run. Exercising outside in the fresh air is very beneficial.

This will keep us physically fit (which improves mental fitness) but, crucially, it will also burn off any stress chemicals that are building up in the body and reduce the chances of any stress induced illness developing.

It's also important to look after our diet as this feeds our body AND our mind.

Make sure you have a balanced food diet including lots of fruit and vegetables. Try to restrict your intake of high fat or high sugar food. Use these as treats rather than regular items on your plate.

One mistake that people often make is not paying attention to what they drink. Things like tea, coffee, coca-cola and energy drinks contain a drug called caffeine. Caffeine is a stimulant and too much of it is very bad for you.

Sugar is also a stimulant so any sugary drinks such as Fanta, Coke and energy drinks (again) are also bad for you.

Too much sugar raises your blood sugar levels. This causes your pancreas to produce too much insulin which can, in time, lead to Type 2 Diabetes. Too many sugary drinks also affect our body at a cellular level allowing the development of problems like cancer, kidney disease, heart disease, brittle bone disease, asthma and even brain damage.

As if that wasn't serious enough it makes our body age faster and, in teenagers it also causes weight gain, many more spots and a dull complexion.

I hope that you can see from this list that drinking any kind of sugary drink is a big no-no and should be avoided at all costs. Energy drinks are now banned from sale to children under 16. This is because it has been medically proven that they stunt growth.

Older teenagers need to know that alcohol can also be very dangerous – not just for the reasons you might be familiar with in terms of being drunk and not being aware of what you are doing or of what others are doing to you – but also because alcohol is a depressant and will increase any feelings of sadness or anxiety.

The Mind

Our mind (the software that runs our brain) is essentially split into two parts.

The Conscious Mind

If you think of the brain like a computer, the conscious mind is the keyboard, the touch screen and the mouse. In other words, it's how we get commands into the computer. Your conscious mind is YOU. It is every thought you will ever have, every decision you will ever make and every action you will ever take. But it is not very powerful. In fact, it only represents about 5% of the power of your brain.

The Subconscious Mind

The subconscious mind is the computer processor – the bit that does all the really powerful work. It keeps your heart beating, keeps you breathing, allows you to walk without thinking (once you've learned how, of course) and so on.

More importantly though, it follows the commands issued by your conscious mind. So, if you say, "I can't do that" or "I'm not good enough" (think back to the chapter about negative self-talk) then your subconscious mind will follow that command and ensure that you can't do it and that you aren't good enough.

This doesn't mean that your subconscious follows every command – it's even more dangerous than that! Your subconscious always follows your strongest thoughts. So, if you think to yourself "I can do this" but you don't really believe it then in the back of your mind you will still be saying "I can't do this" over and over again. This negative belief is more powerful and so it is the one that your subconscious will follow.

That's why we must always re-tune our negative self-talk in a positive but realistic way. Something that we can fully believe AND that will make us feel better, e.g. "I can't do this yet".

So, let's just think about that for a moment. Ninety five percent of the power of your brain treats your strongest thoughts as commands. This means that you are, quite literally, programming yourself for success or failure, positivity or negativity.

One more thing about the subconscious – it NEVER sleeps. Ever.

While the conscious brain is sleeping, the subconscious spends all night processing what you have done during the day. It also means that if you are worrying or stressing about something then your subconscious will continue this worry and stress all night – potentially sending you in and out of fight or flight mode all night. This is where poor sleep patterns come from: we go to bed worrying, we go into fight or flight mode, our body floods with adrenaline, glucose, cortisol – we get nightmares, or we wake up in the middle of the night or we sleep all night, but it is fitful and we wake up feeling exhausted.

Does any of this sound familiar? Having 95% of your brain always switched on is exhausting so it is extremely important that we learn how to relax properly.

Relaxation

Relaxation is not as simple as you might think it is.

You now know that your mind is very busy when you are asleep, so sleeping is not relaxing (for the mind anyway).

When you watch TV or read, your mind is actively engaged in these processes so, whilst they may feel relaxing, they're not relaxing for your mind.

Some people like to walk or do some form of exercise to relax but, if you are thinking about a problem you have or you're mentally running through something that you need to do then, once again, your mind is not relaxing.

So what exactly is relaxation?

Well, personally, I think there are different forms of relaxation and, therefore, there are a number of things that we can do to help our mind to relax and also to feel more relaxed (less stressed) about life in general.

1. Adopt an attitude of gratitude

In today's society it is normal to always want more; I have a super-fast smart phone but now I'd like a super, super fast smart phone, I have a designer t-shirt but I really want a designer fleece and so on.

There is nothing wrong with this type of thinking, in fact, it is good to have something to aim for. But, the downside of this is that it can make us feel as if we never quite have enough or are never quite good enough.

Taking some time out, every day, to reflect on the things we DO have is hugely rewarding. It doesn't always have to be material things (belongings) either; it can be family, friends, a sunny day, a nice experience, anything really.

I would recommend that you take two or three minutes out every morning to say thank you for the things in your life that you are grateful for.

It has a huge positive impact on your mental wellbeing and it puts life into perspective. It can get rid of small day-to-day annoyances that we often get tied up with; being impatient, judging others, being angry and so on. It helps us to be less selfish and to increase our feelings of wellbeing, belonging and connection to others.

I found some wonderful research on the 'Psychology Today' website. It said that there have been a lot of scientific studies done over the last decade and that these show multiple reasons for developing an attitude of gratitude including...

Don't be bitter about what you don't have... ...be thankful for what you do.

- Gratitude helps you feel content. Practicing gratitude is one of the best ways to increase contentment and life satisfaction. It also improves mood by enhancing feelings of optimism, joy, pleasure, enthusiasm, and other positive emotions. Gratitude also reduces anxiety and depression.

- Gratitude promotes physical health. Studies suggest gratitude helps to lower blood pressure, strengthen the immune system, reduce symptoms of illness, and make us less bothered by aches and pains.

- Gratitude improves sleep. Grateful people tend to get more sleep each night, spend less time awake before falling asleep, and feel more rested when they wake up. If you want to sleep more soundly, instead of counting sheep - count your blessings.

- Gratitude strengthens relationships. It makes us feel closer and more connected to friends and boyfriends/girlfriends. When friends feel and express gratitude for each other, they each become more satisfied with their relationship.

- Gratitude encourages "paying it forward." Grateful people are generally more helpful, generous of spirit, and compassionate. These qualities often spill over onto others.

2. Choosing Feelings

I think it would be fair to say that there are many mornings when we wake up and immediately think negatively: "Ugh, it's raining", "Don't want to go to school", "It's too cold, I don't want to get up", "I've got maths today – I hate maths!"

All perfectly normal, of course, but the problem is – negative thoughts lead to negative feelings and before you know it, your day is going badly before you even get out of bed!!!

How much better would it be to start each day feeling positive. Imagine how much more you could achieve in a day. Well, the good news is – you choose your thoughts and feelings... YOU CHOOSE.

I know you may want to challenge this; "Don't be daft! I would never choose to feel bad". And maybe you're right. So, if you do feel bad, what does that mean? It means you are not choosing. So, I will set you a challenge – choose three positive feelings for each day before you get out of bed.

These could be very generic: I feel loved, I feel loving, etc. Or they could be very specific: I am excited about PE today, I feel lucky to have my dog – I'm going to take her for a walk after school today, etc.

On days where you wake up feeling tired, or you have stuff to do that you don't enjoy, it can be quite hard to find three positive feelings for the day. BUT, the rewards are enormous. The positive feelings will shift your focus and remind you that you have many good things in life. The positive feelings will lift your spirits and enable you to deal with whatever the day has to throw at you in a much more constructive way.

There is a wonderful book called *'The Art of Being Brilliant'* by Andy Cope. In this book he talks about the '2 percenters'; the 2 percent of our population who always seem to succeed, to be happy, to have energy.

The amazing news is that you don't have to be rich, you don't need connections, you don't need qualifications to be one of life's '2 percenters'. You just have to choose.

Can you think of anyone who you would describe as a '2 percenter'?

Take a moment to think about it and note down your answers. At the end of this chapter, I have given my best example.

3. Setting Daily Goals

Earlier we looked at the importance of setting goals to achieve balance in our lives. Goal setting can also be used to help us to relax and to help us to feel in control of our lives.

My husband, Tony, is a lovely man: he works hard, he is very supportive and very loving. But, like anyone else, he can become angry when things get too much for him.

He works from home and I don't. I spend a lot of my time travelling to schools or businesses to deliver my training courses and sometimes this also means staying away from home for days at a time. Consequently, Tony not only works from home, but he also does most of the work of running the home.

Most mornings (when I'm at home) we discuss what we have planned for the day. Tony is a graphic designer, so he will tell me about the design jobs he has queued up. Often, when he is finished I will ask him to do a couple of 'home' things.

I might say "Please remember that Jamie (our youngest son) has a dentist appointment today. You'll need to collect him from school". He'll smile and say "OK, no problem". Then I might remember that we have run out of eggs and ask him to go to the shop. Again, he will smile and say "no problem".

Then just as I am leaving I might mention that the bins need to be emptied.

At that point it will all get too much and he shouts "Right then, I'll add that to my to do list, shall I?!"

From nice to not so nice in just one step. But why? It's got nothing to do with the bins, that's for sure.

Basically, it's because he has gone from feeling 'in control' to feeling 'out of control' because I have asked him to remember to do too many things at once.

The brain is a super-complicated organ. In addition to everything I have already told you about it, it also has many different types of memory.

The memory we use when we are trying to remember things 'in the moment' is called working memory. This is what we use to pay attention to and manipulate information coming in to our conscious mind.

For years and years, I have told students that we can only process 7 pieces of information at one time but, more recently there have been some studies that suggest working memory can actually only deal with just three or four things at once. When this limit is reached, we forget stuff and 'lose control'.

Nobody enjoys feeling out of control and so this leads to negative behaviours such as anger, fear and upset. And, as you know, these behaviours put us into fight or flight mode which reduces our ability to think straight and to control our emotions and so the negative cycle begins again. Round and around we go. So, how can setting daily goals help us?

It's simple really. They give us control.

Useful Tip

It's a really good idea to keep a notebook by your bed. If you wake up during the night worrying about something or, mentally noting that you need to do something, if you quickly write it down then your mind can relax and you will be able to go back to sleep. In the morning, you can simply add whatever it is to your to do list.

Instead of calling them goals, let's just call it a **to-do list** (or a 'Get Done' list as one of my friends likes to say).

Writing down the things we need to do that day gives us control. We no longer need to try and remember things in our head and when someone asks us to do something else we simply add it to the list.

Seeing your tasks written down also gives you the ability to prioritise things so that if you can't get everything done in one day, you can at least ensure that you get the most important things done.

Ticking things off the list gives us a feeling of achievement too which boosts our confidence and makes us feel better about ourselves.

Anything left on the list at the end of the day is simply transferred onto the list for tomorrow.

Remember to include items on your to do list that relate to the bigger goals – the targets that you set yourself in the Big Top Model. This will help you to progress towards them and to feel good about yourself.

4. Meditation

Historically, meditation has been linked to religion and also to specific poses (like sitting with your legs crossed and chanting). It is true that these are both examples of different types of meditation. HOWEVER!!!! These images, unfortunately just get in the way of our understanding of what meditation actually is and how it can benefit our mental (and physical) wellbeing.

Meditation is actually the process of training your mind to focus and redirect your thoughts and you can use it in all sorts of useful ways including: increasing awareness of yourself, reducing stress and developing concentration. And it doesn't end there!

Meditation can also be used to develop good habits and feelings, positive mood, positive outlook, self-discipline, good sleep patterns and even an increased tolerance to pain – not bad really when all you have to do is sit or lie comfortably for a few minutes each day.

So, let's have a closer look at the many, many benefits of meditation – and then we'll look at how simple it is to do.

- Meditation reduces stress

As you know, our brain releases cortisol when we are stressed.
Increased levels of cortisol can disrupt sleep, increase blood
pressure, cloud our thinking, lead to mental health issues such as
depression and anxiety and it can make us feel less energetic.

Studies show that regular meditation carried out over eight weeks
reduces the effects caused by cortisol and can also reduce symptoms
in people who have medical conditions triggered by stressful
situations.

- Meditation controls anxiety

As stress levels reduce so do
anxiety levels. Meditation also
reduces symptoms of more
serious anxiety disorders including
phobias, paranoia, OCD and panic
attacks.

Longer term studies have shown
that people who continue
meditating after the first eight
weeks maintain lower anxiety
levels.

Taking control

My own son uses meditation
every day to control his anxiety
and to control the onset of
panic attacks and seizures.
Our doctor is ecstatic that
he is using such a positive
technique to stay healthy. All
he does is lie on his bed and
listen to some calming music
for 10 minutes. So easy, but
so effective!

Meditation isn't always just about sitting or lying down. Techniques
like Yoga and Tai Chi can be a form of meditation and have also been
shown to reduce anxiety.

- Meditation promotes emotional health

Some forms of meditation can lead to improved self-image. From the
Big Top Model exercise, we learned how important a positive self-
image is in building our resilience. Meditation also gives us a more

positive outlook on life. Long term meditation practise has been proven to reduce depression too!

• Meditation enhances self-awareness

Meditation can help you to develop a stronger understanding of yourself helping you to be your best self. For example, self-inquiry meditation specifically aims to help you understand yourself better and how you relate to others around you.

Other styles teach you to recognise thoughts that might be harmful to you. As you become more familiar with your thought habits you can begin to steer them in a more positive direction. Meditation also helps us to become more creative at problem solving.

• Meditation increases attention span

Focussed-attention (like concentrating on your breathing) meditation is a bit like weight-lifting for your attention span. It helps to increase the strength and endurance of your concentration. It has also been shown to improve memory and it reverses brain patterns that contribute to mind-wandering and worrying.

One study found that meditating for just four days in a row was enough to increase attention span! Perfect for those lovely pre-exam revision sessions.

• Meditation may reduce age-related memory loss

OK, so as a teenager, you may not be worried about this just yet – but your parents certainly will be!

Through improving your attention abilities and your clarity of thinking you will help your mind to stay young.

This is where the 'chanting' styles of meditation come in useful. They combine a mantra (or a chant) with repetitive finger movements to focus thoughts which leads to improved performance in memory tasks among older people.

Meditation has also been shown to partially improve memory in patients with dementia.

● Meditation can generate kindness

Metta meditation is a Buddhist-based meditation for cultivating compassion and forgiveness. It begins with developing kind thoughts and feeling towards yourself. With practise, you can then extend these thoughts to the people around you - beginning with friends and family and, eventually, even extending to enemies.

With Metta meditation you are rewarded exponentially for your efforts – the more time you put into it, the better the results you attain.

Other benefits of Metta meditation include reducing social anxiety, reducing relationship conflicts and helping with anger management.

● Meditation may help fight addictions

Because regular meditation helps you to develop mental discipline, you can then use this to increase your self-control and your awareness of the triggers that lead to addictive behaviours.

Research has shown that meditation can help to increase will-power, control emotions and increase understanding of the causes behind addictive behaviours. Meditation can also help you to lose weight and eliminate other unwanted habits.

• Meditation improves sleep

Sleep is as important to the health of our brain as oxygen is to the health of our body.

And yet, almost half of the population will struggle with insomnia (difficulty sleeping) at some point.

One study that compared a group of people who meditated and another group who didn't showed that the meditators fell asleep faster and stayed asleep for longer.

Being skilled in meditation helps you to control your thoughts and avoid the 'mind-racing' that is often linked to insomnia.

• Meditation helps control pain

When we are stressed we feel pain more acutely as we are more aware of it.

Using MRI scans it has been proven that the parts of our brain that control pain become stronger with as little as four days of meditation. This results in reduced sensitivity to pain.

Some studies even show that meditation can help to reduce chronic pain in people with terminal illnesses.

Stay well.

Sleep is to the brain as oxygen is to the body.

- Meditation can reduce blood pressure

Again, maybe this is one that would interest adults more than teenagers, but everyone becomes an adult eventually!

When we go into fight or flight mode our blood pressure rises. Over time this can lead to heart problems and strokes. Studies show that meditation appears to control blood pressure and the signals that trigger fight or flight. Not only does blood pressure reduce during actual meditation sessions, it reduces overall in people who practise regularly.

- Meditation – The Bottom Line

Meditation is something that anyone can do to improve their mental and emotional health.

Most forms of meditation don't need special equipment or space and you can do it for just a few minutes each day, so it doesn't take up a lot of time either.

In the eye of a storm all is still and quiet. When you encounter your own personal storms, find your still an quiet centre and stay there until the storm has passed.

There are loads of fantastic apps available (most of them for free) where you can try different styles depending on what you want to achieve. I would recommend 'Headspace' as a good introduction. The first ten sessions are free and you'll get a good idea of what's involved.

You can choose to use meditation to clear your mind and relax or to become more self-aware – to get to know yourself better and to become calmer and more confident.

I even used a form of meditation to enable me to walk 20 metres over red-hot coals!

5. Screen Time

Reducing the amount of time we spend on screens (TV, Computers, Phone) helps us to be more relaxed. This is particularly important in the evening, before we go to bed.

Screens (and energy efficient bulbs) emit light on the blue wavelength. This type of light has been scientifically proven to disrupt our brain's ability to produce melatonin.

Melatonin is the body's natural sleep chemical.

The body operates on something called the circadian rhythm – this is our biological clock. The circadian rhythm is affected by light.

Before we had artificial lighting, our body clock responded to the natural light around us – keeping us awake and alert during daylight and preparing us for sleep (by producing melatonin) in the evening when it was darker.

Now, though, we are surrounded by bright lights most of the time. In the evening light of any kind disrupts our body clock but, light on the blue wavelength is by far the worst.

NB. Blue light isn't always bad. During the day it boosts attention, reaction time and mood.

Science suggests that we need to stop looking at blue light up to three hours before bedtime to maintain our natural circadian rhythm. In the modern world, this is probably a little unrealistic.

I always recommend moderation.

In my family, my kids have to switch off computers etc. an hour before bedtime. They use this time to shower, read (or other non-screen related activities) and meditate. For my older son, in particular, this has significantly improved his sleep patterns.

6. Sleep

Good sleep patterns are SO important for our health and yet they are often the first thing to be disturbed when we are feeling low, angry, stressed, worried, excited and any number of other emotions.

We can see from the earlier parts of this chapter that there are a number of things we can do to help:

- Turn off screens one hour before bed
- Do not use any night lights
- Meditate before bedtime
- Keep a positivity journal
- Keep a notebook by your bed for midnight niggling thoughts

If you've done all of this though and you are still having trouble sleeping there is also a holistic breathing technique that can help you fall asleep in around a minute.

It is called the '4-7-8' exercise and is championed by the best-selling author Dr Andrew Weil.

The 4-7-8 Exercise

1. Place the tip of your tongue on the tissue ridge on your upper front teeth and keep it there throughout the exercise.

2. Exhale through your mouth making a 'whoosh' sound as you do

3. Close your mouth and slowly breathe in through your nose for a count of four

4. Hold your breath for a count of seven

5. Breathe out for a count of eight making the same 'whoosh' noise again

6. Repeat four times

7. Sweet dreams

The Spirit

Looking after your body and your mind are really important in building and maintaining resilience but, equally important, is the need to look after your spirit.

This doesn't mean being spiritual or religious (although these things help many millions of people). In this instance I am talking about your general feelings of happiness and contentment. Your ability to look after 'Number 1' first, to be kind and caring to yourself, to do the things that make you feel good and to reflect on all of the positives in your life.

You matter more than anyone!

Have you ever been in an aeroplane? If so, you will have seen the safety demonstration where they show you the emergency exits, the brace position and so on. They also say that "if the oxygen masks fall from the panel above you must fit your own mask first". Why do they say this?

Surely, if you're with a small child or someone vulnerable, you would want to make sure that they are okay first, wouldn't you? It's only natural. But, the truth is, if you can't breathe properly while you're trying to do this then you won't be able to help them, AND you won't be able to help yourself either.

It is vital that we look after ourselves first. Only by doing this can we be strong enough to help the others around us.

Take time to nurture yourself.

Life today is busy, busy, busy. It's full of all kinds of pressures at school, at home, with relationships, responsibilities, staying healthy and so the list goes on.

It is really important to take some time for yourself just to have fun or to relax. This could be something as simple as listening to some music that you enjoy, doing some meditation, having a bath, spending time with friends, watching your favourite TV programme, eating your favourite food, playing your favourite sport – I'm sure you get the idea.

Sadly though, these are often the things that get neglected when we are busy or under pressure and yet, without them, we begin to feel quite low and this can lead to all kinds of issues.

Even if you are in the middle of studying for important exams it is still important to take a little time out for yourself each day.

Keep a positivity journal

Earlier in this chapter we spoke about having an 'attitude of gratitude' and how saying thank you each day can have a very positive impact on our wellbeing.

A positivity journal is a similar concept and equally simple. All you have to do, at the end of each day, is to reflect back on your day and write down the three most positive things that happened.

Maybe you made someone smile, maybe someone made you smile. Was the sun shining, did school go particularly well, did you have something nice to eat, did you achieve something that made you feel happy or proud?

It can be anything at all.

The important thing is that you do it every day and that you write it down. Because of the way our memory works, just thinking about it isn't good enough as we will have forgotten most of it by the next day.

Typing it into your phone or tablet won't work because these are screens and we need to avoid screens at night.

If you can, buy yourself a small notebook or journal (if not, any little book will do – even one made out of scrap paper) and simply write down your positives last thing each night before you go to sleep. This will make you feel good and it will also ensure that your sub-conscious is thinking about nice things whilst you are sleeping.

Importantly though, as your positivity journal grows it becomes a fantastic support tool. Any time you are feeling down you can simply look back at all of the positives in your life and it helps to keep everything in perspective. It's a win-win!

Woah! Isn't that a lot to do every day?

Actually, no. It's a whole lot simpler than it looks. We've even designed a little template to help you. It's called the 'Daily Workout'.

You can download free copies of the 'Daily Workout' from our website *www.resilientme.co.uk/resources.*

It's really simple to use and, if you want to, you can build it into your positivity journal to keep everything in the same place. This is just one suggestion and it's the way I use the 'Daily Workout' to fit it easily in to my life.

In the morning, when I wake up, I press the snooze button just once. During this time, I think of three things that I would like to say 'thank you' for and I think of three positive feelings for the day. Then I start to make a mental note of my goals (or to do list) for the day.

When the alarm goes off again, I get up and write these things straight into my journal.

This way, I start every day in a positive frame of mind and in control. Then I just get on with my day.

In the evening, once all the screens are switched off, I reflect back on the day and write down anything I have achieved for my mind, my body and my spirit. If I haven't achieved something for all of these, it doesn't matter. Writing it down just helps me to keep track of how well I am looking after myself.

Finally, I write down three positives from the day and then I do 10 minutes of meditation which helps me to relax and go to sleep quickly and easily.

The whole process, including meditation, takes no more than 20 minutes spread throughout my whole day.

My Favourite 2 Percenter

My favourite 2 percenter is Richard Branson. Always smiling, always full of energy, always looking for the next challenge, never afraid to take risks, always learning from his mistakes.

Did you know that Richard Branson is dyslexic, but his first successful business venture was producing a college magazine. He never lets personal difficulties stand in his way.

Another favourite of mine is Will.I.am. Always full of energy, always enthusiastic, always trying to help build other people up, never afraid to try something new. Will comes from a very impoverished background and suffers from ADHD but, again, he never lets any of that stand in his way.

- We need to look after our wellbeing on a daily basis taking a holistic approach that covers mind, body and spirit

- For the body we need to
    - Do cardio exercise for 20 minutes 5 times a week
    - Eat a healthy, balanced diet
    - Be careful with drinks – avoid caffeine, sugar and alcohol
    - Be aware of the damage that drugs can cause

- Our mind is split into two sections
    - The conscious brain is YOU, everything you think, say and do. It represents only 5% of the power of your mind
    - The subconscious mind is like a supercomputer that processes all of your thoughts. It represents 95% of your mind and can be used to programme yourself for success or failure based on your thoughts and feelings

- The subconscious mind NEVER sleeps so we must learn how to relax and switch off to give ourselves a break

- Having an attitude of gratitude helps us to be less selfish and to increase our feelings of wellbeing, belonging and connection to others

- Choose THREE positive feelings for each day before you get out of bed. This will shift your focus and remind you that you have many good things in life. It will also lift your spirits and enable you to deal with whatever the day has to throw at you in a much more constructive way.

- We need to look after our wellbeing on a daily basis taking a holistic approach that covers mind, body and spirit

- For the body we need
    - Cardio exercise for 20 minutes 5 times a week
    - Eat a healthy, balanced diet
    - Be careful with drinks – avoid caffeine, sugar and alcohol
    - Be aware of the damage that drugs can cause

- Set goals for yourself everyday – some of this will just be a to do list but be sure to include tasks that will help you to achieve the targets you set in the Big Top Model.
    - This will help you to feel in control
    - This will help you to achieve and progress

- Meditation is something that anyone can do to improve their mental and emotional health. You don't need special equipment or space and you can do it for just a few minutes each day. It has many benefits including
    - Reducing stress
    - Controlling anxiety
    - Promoting emotional health
    - Enhancing self-awareness
    - Increasing attention span
    - Reducing age-related memory loss
    - Can generate kindness
    - Can help fight addiction
    - Improving sleep
    - Helping control pain
    - Reducing blood pressure

- Try an app such as Headspace to get you started

- Screens (and energy efficient bulbs) emit light on the blue wavelength. This type of light has been scientifically proven to disrupt our brain's ability to produce melatonin which is our natural sleep chemical

- Good sleep patterns are essential for our emotional and physical well-being.
    - Turn off screens one hour before bed
    - Do not use any night lights
    - Meditate before bedtime
    - Keep a positivity journal
    - Keep a notebook by your bed
    - Practise the 4-7-8 exercise

- Look after yourself first. This will also help you to look after the people you care about

- Take time to nurture yourself by doing something 'just for you' every single day

- Keep a positivity journal – every evening, write down three positives from your day. You could keep a special journal for writing these positives down and read through it from time to time to feel just how positive your life really is

- Complete the 'Daily Workout' each day

'Awesome' ends in 'me'.

Anon

GRADUATION

Whoop whoop. Congratulations!

Time to grab your cape and mortar board -
and let's bring on the clowns!

Congratulations! You are now a graduate of 'The Circus of Life'.

BALANCE
You know how to balance four key areas of your life – school or college work, independent learning, being healthy and having fun!

JUGGLING
You know how to juggle three of life's most important skills – Resilience, Growth and Wellbeing

TIGHTROPE WALKING
You know how to set goals and stay focussed on the way ahead, managing wobbles along the way.

TRAPEZE
Believe in yourself, fly as high as you want to and use support when you need it

FIRE EATING
You know that opportunity is always there – failure is only failure when we give up or don't try at all.

Along the way you have learned about what stress is and how a little bit of stress can be good as it motivates us. We also looked at how too much stress can have a very negative impact on our life.

Now we understand our 'fight or flight' response and how it is designed to protect us but also how, over time, we can get stuck in fight or flight mode and this can lead to stress induced illness – both physical and mental.

We looked at our beautiful brain and saw how the power of positive thinking can program us for success in life (and how negative thinking can make life worse for us).

We learned how to use the 'Big Top Model'. This is a fantastic tool that helps us to:

- monitor our internal chatter, turning negative thoughts into powerful, positive statements
- build a positive self-image
- understand the importance of a growth mindset
- monitor the balance in our life
- set goals
- coach ourselves to success and, most importantly
- identify WHY we want to do all these things

The Big Top Model is not a one-off exercise though, it is a tool that we can use over and over again to build ourselves up and to feel at our best.

We also know now that we need to look after ourselves every day.

- **Physically**, through looking after our diet, sleeping well and exercising regularly
- **Mentally**, through practising an 'attitude of gratitude', starting our day by choosing positive thoughts and feelings, taking control of our day using 'to do lists', relaxing and focussing the mind with meditation, being mindful of how much time we spend looking at screens and remembering to switch them off an hour before bedtime and adopting good sleep habits
- **Spiritually**, by putting yourself first, making time to do things that make you feel happy and keeping a positivity diary

It all sounds complicated and time consuming, but we've made it super-simple through the use of our 'Daily Workout'.

Together, all these things will help us to feel good about ourselves, to reach for – and achieve – success in our lives and will give us the strength we need to adjust to, and to deal with, the difficulties that life will throw at us.

This is called Resilience.

One last word...

No circus would be complete without the clowns whose sole purpose is to make us laugh. Laughter is one of the greatest resilience tools of all time. In fact, laughter has been proven to reduce our stress, reduce our blood pressure and to boost our immune system. What other reasons do you need?

Laugh. Laugh. And laugh some more.

THE CIRCUS OF LIFE

This is to certify that on the

_____ day of _____

_____

graduated with honours from the Circus of Life

The Ringmaster

"Today this could be the greatest day of our lives"

Take That

THE ENCORE

As often happens at the end of a
performance, the audience yells for more.

No show would be complete without the extra bits at the end, so here they are...

Earlier in this book we looked at how our own internal chatter can make us feel really bad. We call this negative self-talk. But, we also looked at how to recognise this negativity when it is happening and learned to re-tune to a more positive, helpful wavelength.

Here are some examples of how to re-tune everyday negativity....

NEGATIVE SELF-TALK		POSITIVE RE-TUNE
I can't do that	→	I can't do that yet
There's too much to do	→	I need to break it down into tasks and prioritise them
There isn't enough time	→	I will do the most important task first
I don't enjoy this	→	How will I benefit from doing this?
I can't do anything about it	→	I will take control of the areas I can, and I will stop worrying about the ones that I can't
I'm too fat/thin	→	Which parts of my body do I like?
I'm not as pretty/handsome as XXX	→	What's the nicest thing about me?
Why does this happen to me?	→	Why not? What can I do about it?

These examples are not the 'right' answers. They are simply examples. The 'right' answer is the one that makes YOU feel better about a difficult situation or makes YOU feel more in control.

Feeling 'out of control' is one of the quickest ways to feel stressed and, therefore, to trigger your fight-or-flight response.

Mental health is no different to physical health. Both go up and down all the time and this just means we are normal.

Sometimes we feel okay and other times we can feel really sad, sometimes we feel as fit as a fiddle and other times we suffer from a cold or something worse.

Sometimes though, mental health is something that you may need help with from a doctor or another professional – in the same way as you would need help if you had a problem with your heart.

'Mental' health just means that it is your brain that needs some help – and remember, the brain is just an organ, the same as your heart, your lungs, your liver and so on.

The problem though, is that our brain is the central processor of our body (just like the CPU in a computer). When something is affecting your CPU – everything else is affected too. This doesn't mean that you are weak, it means you've caught a metaphorical virus, like a computer. And we all know that when our computer gets a virus it needs to be dealt with.

Mental Health issues can occur in anybody at any time and can be triggered by any number of factors at home or at school. However, unlike a physical illness, mental health issues are not always visible and, because of this, can become serious before they are detected and diagnosed.

23% of teenagers will experience a mental health issue before they reach the age of 20.

Many different things can increase the risk of a teenager developing a mental health issue including bullying, cyberbullying, peer pressure, exam pressure, physical disability, sexuality, friendship issues, family issues, distressing events, ethnicity, poverty, mental disabilities such as autism or ADHD, poor self-image, negative self-talk and so the list goes on.

We know from our earlier chapter on stress that every time we feel powerful negative emotions, we trigger our fight or flight response. In turn, this releases chemicals in our body that can build up and attack our organs. If that organ happens to be your brain, then this may lead to a mental health issue.

But, don't worry, if you know how to spot the signs AND you follow everything you have been taught about resilience, then you can protect yourself and help everyone else around you too.

There are a number of different mental health categories including Depression, Anxiety, Eating Disorders, Psychosis and Suicide. Even though each category is different, there are some common behaviours that might be a sign, or a symptom, of a developing mental health issue.

These include:

- Feeling sad or withdrawn for a long time
- Taking extreme risks – either physical or verbal (like yelling at a teacher)
- Experiencing intense worries or fears
- Not eating or becoming obsessed with exercise
- Hurting yourself deliberately or thinking about suicide
- Severe mood swings that are bad enough to affect friendships and relationships
- Using drugs or drinking alcohol
- Sudden, overwhelming fear
- Changes in your behaviour, in your personality or in your sleeping patterns.

We will ALL experience some of these things some of the time. This does NOT mean that everyone has a mental health problem. Most of the time it just means we are normal. However, if some, or all of these things are happening frequently or lasting for a long time then they may be warning signs that you need to go and tell someone about.

In the next few appendices we will explain what each different category is so that you might spot the danger signs in yourself, or in others. Of course, if you suspect something is wrong you should tell someone straight away – no matter what!

Depression isn't just sadness. Everyone gets sad or feels 'the blues' from time to time.

Even the word 'depression' can mean different things depending on the situation. When you are really busy or under a lot of pressure – maybe during exam periods – it is normal to feel 'stressed out'. It's also perfectly normal to feel down if you've had some kind of setback, negative or even traumatic, experience.

Depression affects everyone differently and the symptoms range from mild to severe – ranging from feeling low all the time to feeling suicidal.

Clinical depression – feeling low persistently for at least two weeks - has an affect on how we behave, how we feel (physically and mentally) and even how we think.

It can be hard to identify depression because life always has 'ups and downs' and everyone has times when they don't feel at their best.

Someone with depression may feel sad, anxious, worried, guilty, self-critical or even angry or helpless. Often, they will feel confused and find it difficult to make decisions. It could be hard to concentrate on things and, at its worst, they may even have suicidal thoughts.

It is common to lack energy, to feel demotivated and to feel very tired most (or all) of the time. It is also common to lose interest in things like appearance and responsibilities.

Sufferers may cry more often, feel more achy, withdraw from social situations and they may even adopt behaviours such as self-harming, taking risks, abusing alcohol or drugs and either over or under-eating.

Sometimes you can notice depression by the way that people talk. For example, they might say things like "I'm a failure", "It's all my fault", "It's hopeless", "I'm worthless", "No-one can help", "It's never going to get better" or even "Life isn't worth living".

If you notice these signs and symptoms in yourself then you should go and talk to a medical professional. Depression is a real illness (it's not just 'in your head') and it can be treated. Just like any other illness, the sooner it is treated, the sooner you will get better!

If you think one of your friends or someone in your family is suffering, encourage them to talk about it and to go and ask for help.

Appendix D – What is anxiety?

Everyone feels anxious at some point. It is a natural response and helps to protect us from danger. Most teenagers worry about things like exams or friendships, but once the difficulty has passed they feel okay again.

Anxiety disorders are something different and are often triggered by stress. Whilst anxiety is usually in response to outside events and forces, it is possible to create an anxiety disorder through negative self-talk – in other words, people who always tell themselves the worst will happen (remember we spent time looking at this in the Big Top Model).

Anxiety is a feeling of fear or panic, stress, tension or worry that can become a mental health issue if you are feeling this way all or most of the time. Anxiety is very common with just under 20% of young people experiencing it at any one time.

An anxiety disorder makes it difficult, or impossible, to do the things you normally like doing or are able to do.

As well as general anxiety there are a number of different types of anxiety disorder and more than one can be experienced at the same time. These include

- Panic disorder - when you experience panic attacks
- Social phobia - where you fear social situations
- Obsessive Compulsive disorder (OCD) - when people feel compelled to perform repetitive behaviours
- Post Traumatic Stress disorder (PTSD) – some people experience this after witnessing or suffering a life-threatening event

Anxiety problems are one of the most common mental health issues, and it is also very common to experience a mixture of anxiety and depression. Just like depression, anxiety is a real illness, it is not something that's just "in your head" or that you can just "snap out of" (people who say these kinds of things are just lacking knowledge in this area). And, just like depression, anxiety can be treated.

So, how would you spot anxiety? Well, someone with anxiety may feel scared, worried, on edge or nervous a lot of the time. They might find it hard to concentrate, constantly overthinking things or having mental blocks, making it difficult to make decisions. Often this can result in feelings of anger, confusion, irritability, impatience and restlessness. Sleep can be affected by vivid dreams leading to tiredness and, sometimes, unwanted, unpleasant, repetitive thoughts.

People with anxiety often want to avoid or escape from social situations as they may find them extremely distressing. Some sufferers adopt repetitive compulsive behaviours that can become phobic.

Anxiety can be very physical with symptoms including dry mouth, palpitations, hyperventilating and chest pains. It is common to feel, or be, sick or to have diarrhoea. In some cases, there may also be panic attacks or blackouts.

If you notice these signs and symptoms in yourself then you should go and talk to a medical professional. Do not be scared – anxiety is just an illness and it can be treated – the sooner, the better!

If you think one of your friends or someone in your family is suffering, encourage them to talk about it and to go and ask for help.

Panic Attacks

A panic attack is when feelings of anxiety become intense and overwhelming. The person will normally experience physical symptoms including shortness of breath, sweating, an increased heartbeat or blurry vision. A panic attack can be associated with a particular place, object or situation. Some people find the thought of having a panic attack itself is a trigger.

Lots of people have different eating habits but just because you sometimes diet or sometimes eat too much doesn't mean you have a problem. It's when behaviour around food is more extreme that there may be an issue.

An eating disorder is a mental health illness where food is used to try and manage feelings. Sometimes eating disorders are triggered by worrying about body image but they can also be triggered when you are stressed, worried or when other areas of your life feel out of control. Being able to control what you eat can give you back that feeling of order.

There are a large number of different types of eating disorder including:

- *Anorexia Nervosa* – when you try to keep your weight as low as possible by not eating enough food, by exercising too much, or both

- *Bulimia* – when you regularly eat too much at one time and then make yourself sick. Bulimics might also use laxatives (to make them poo a lot) or exercise too much

- *Binge Eating Disorder (BED)* – when you often eat far too much, feel physically uncomfortable and then feel really guilty

- *Eating Disorder Not Otherwise Specified (EDNOS)* – when your symptoms don't match any of the other disorders exactly, but you may still have a very serious problem

EDNOS is the most common eating disorder (though most people have not even heard of it) and anorexia is the least common (though nearly everyone knows about it).

Some of the signs of a possible eating disorder can include:
- Losing your appetite
- Eating, even when you are not hungry
- Being obsessed with your body image (too fat, too thin, not muscular enough etc.)
- Following fad diets or only eating certain foods
- Losing or gaining weight dramatically
- Being afraid of gaining weight
- Making yourself sick after eating

- Hiding food
- Finding it difficult to eat in social situations
- Being secretive around food
- Focussing on buying and cooking food for other people

Even if you have one or more of these symptoms it doesn't mean you definitely have an eating disorder but, if they are affecting your everyday life, you should definitely go and talk to a doctor.

An eating disorder is when you have an unhealthy attitude to food, which can take over your life and make you ill.

Appendix F – What is psychosis?

Psychosis, itself, is not a diagnosable illness. The word is usually used to describe an experience. It can be a symptom of some serious mental health illnesses including bipolar disorder, schizophrenia, paranoid personality disorder, post-partum psychosis or delusional/paranoid disorder.

If someone has a psychotic episode, they lose touch with reality. They might hear voices or have hallucinations (seeing things that aren't there) or delusions (believing things that aren't true). They may also become paranoid or feel that their life is in danger. Sometimes psychosis can cause muddled thinking and difficulty concentrating and can also make you feel as if something else is controlling you.

Even if you are experiencing one or more of these symptoms, it doesn't always mean that you are affected by psychosis. Just like all mental health issues, if you suspect that you may be suffering you should go and talk to someone you trust or to a medical professional.

Psychosis can be scary but, if it is caught early enough, it is treatable and, despite what the media says, the word psychotic does not mean dangerous.

It is also possible to experience psychosis on its own because of other factors including:

- Physical illness or injury – if you have a high fever or a head injury, you may see or hear things. Conditions such as Alzheimer's or Parkinson's can cause hallucinations and delusions

- Drugs – some drugs can cause hallucinations or can make you hear things that aren't there

- Lack of Sleep – this, too, can cause hallucinations

- Hunger – extreme hunger or low blood sugar can cause hallucinations

- Bereavement – sometimes when you have lost someone you love you may hear them talking to you and you may also feel that they are there with you even though you can't see them

- Abuse or Trauma – both of these can cause psychotic episodes

- Spiritual or Religious Experiences – some people hear voices or see visions as part of these types of experience. This can be very positive

- Family – it is possible to inherit psychosis if a blood relative has it

Appendix G – What is suicide?

Suicide is a complicated issue. Not everyone who dies by suicide has been suffering from a mental health issue but they have all been suffering with a great deal of emotional pain.

Some people who are feeling suicidal will ask for help but many don't, and it can be extremely difficult to spot it if the sufferer does not want you to know.

The signs that someone may be feeling suicidal are the same as the common signs for all mental health issues (see Appendix B). In addition to these a suicidal person might display very impulsive behaviour, may start giving possessions away, be extremely secretive or have strange conversations that are about saying 'goodbye' without actually saying it. Sometimes though, a suicidal person will appear very calm and happy. This is because they have already made their decision – what they are going to do and when they are going to do it – and they feel much more in control.

In the UK, suicide rates are highest in men aged 15 – 50. Every year, more men are killed by suicide than by car accidents or even by cancer. The reasons for this are not completely clear but it is suspected that men are less likely to ask for help when they need it and then things just become so bad that they can't see any other options. **But there is always another option!**

Why would someone take their own life?

There are so many different reasons why a teenager may think about, or complete, suicide including:

- mental health problems
- bullying or discrimination
- abuse – sexual or physical
- the death of someone they love
- the end of a relationship
- long-term physical pain or illness
- adjusting to a big change, such as moving house or going to university
- homelessness
- isolation or loneliness
- feeling inadequate or a failure
- losing a loved one to suicide
- addiction or substance abuse
- pregnancy, childbirth or postnatal depression
- cultural pressure, such as forced marriage
- doubts about your sexual or gender identity

What should I do if I feel suicidal?

The answer to this is simple – tell someone. Do not keep suicidal feelings to yourself. Talk to someone you trust (a friend, a teacher, a family member) or go and see your doctor. There are also helplines like 'The Samaritans' that are available 24 hours a day – every day.

What should I do if I suspect that someone I know is suicidal?

I know this may seem strange but, if you suspect that someone is suicidal, the best thing that you can do is ask them. Don't dance around the subject just say something like "Are you thinking of taking your own life?"

Research done by Professor Rory O'Connor (and his team at Glasgow University) shows that asking someone directly about feelings of suicide makes them feel listened to. It also validates their feelings.

At worst, they may laugh at you and say "no". At best, this could be the conversation that saves their life!

Appendix H – Gaming: good or bad?

The International Classification of Diseases (ICD) is a document produced periodically by the World Health Organisation (WHO). The last edition was produced in 1992. The ICD is a guide that doctors use to track and diagnose diseases. In the newest edition (2018) of the ICD, gaming addiction is listed as a mental health condition for the first time. It is known as Gaming Disorder.

> ### Gaming Disorder
>
> A pattern of persistent or recurrent gaming behaviour so severe that it takes precedence over other life interests.
>
> **Symptoms include:**
>
> • Impaired control over gaming (frequency, intensity, duration)
>
> • Increased priority given to gaming
>
> • Continuation or escalation of gaming despite negative consequences

In some ways, this is a good thing. It means that this type of addiction will be taken seriously and that more support will be available. Some countries already restrict the hours that young people can access online games (South Korea, Japan, China), some identify it as a major public health issue and some countries (including the UK) have private "addiction" clinics to treat the condition.

Is it all bad?

Part of Normal Life

At Oxford University a recent study has suggested that young people are not necessarily gaming to the exclusion of everything else, rather that they mix their screen time with daily life, doing things like homework – much like adults using computers at work.

Supporting Poor Mental Health

Also, Johnny Chiodini (a video game producer) argues that some good is done by gaming. He has a YouTube series called 'Low Batteries' that looks at how some people actually use gaming to help them cope with existing mental health struggles. He says that he personally used video games as a support tool whenever his life was difficult and that this helped to stop his internal negative self-talk.

Active involvement – greater understanding

One benefit that gaming offers above TV and books is that players can get actively involved. So, instead of just watching a character deal with a problem, the player actively solves the problem for them, leading to a more in-depth understanding.

For example, there is a game called 'Life is Strange' which allows players to 'walk a mile' in the shoes of someone who has mental health problems. In this game, players control a girl who can rewind time. The story is about how one single action can cause a chain reaction that affects many people. It is about the importance of decision making.

Suicide is one of the issues that it deals with and at the end of difficult scenes it brings up advice and helpline numbers. There was also a TV programme that dealt with suicide called *'13 Reasons Why'*.

A lot of people would argue that being involved in solving the issue (active) rather than just watching someone else go through it (passive) leads to much greater empathy.

So, Good or Bad? My view is that gaming can be both good and bad depending on how it is used. It is definitely a part of modern life that is here to stay, and I believe that like many other things in life that are potentially addictive (food, alcohol, coffee, work) we need to learn to use gaming in moderation.

But also, like any other mental health issue, if you are worried that you (or a friend) may be developing a problem, please go and talk to someone straight away. The sooner you get help, the sooner you will get better.

Anorexia and Bulimia Care www.anorexiabulimiacare.org.uk
If you're being affected by an eating disorder, you can ring the
helpline. Helpline 03000 11 12 13 (option 1: support line, option 2:
family and friends)

Anxiety UK www.anxietyuk.org.uk
08444 775 774 (Mon – Fri 09:30 – 17:30)
Supporting diagnosed sufferers

B-eat www.b-eat.co.uk
If you have an eating disorder, or someone in your family does, b-eat
is the place you can go to for information and support.
*   Helpline number for under 25's: 0808 801 0711 (Daily 3pm-10pm)
*   Email: fyp@b-eat.co.uk
*   To know what local help and support you can get, put your
    postcode into HelpFinder

Big White Wall bigwhitewall.com
Online community for adults experiencing emotional or psychological
distress. It is free to use in many areas if you live in the UK, if you're a
student or if you have a referral from your GP.

CALM
(Campaign Against Living Miserably) www.thecalmzone.net
Offers support to young men in the UK who are down or in a crisis.
*   Helpline: 0800 58 58 58 (Daily 17:00-midnight)
Webchat

Childline www.childline.org.uk
*   If you're under 19 you can confidentially call, email or chat online
    about any problem big or small
*   Freephone 24h helpline: 0800 1111

- Sign up for a childline account on the website to be able to message a counsellor anytime without using your email address

Chat 1:1 with an online advisor

Cruse Bereavement Care cruse.org.uk 0844 477 9400
Charity providing information and support after someone you know has died.

Depression Alliance www.depressionalliance.org
Charity for sufferers of depression

Depression UK depressionuk.org
A self-help organisation made up of individuals and local groups.

Elefriends elefriends.org.uk
Elefriends is a friendly, supportive online community for people experiencing a mental health problem.

Maytree www.maytree.org.uk 0207 263 7070
A sanctuary for the suicidal

Men Get Eating Disorders Too www.mengetedstoo.co.uk
Information and advice for men on eating disorders.

Men's Health Forum www.menshealthforum.org.uk
24/7 stress support for men

Mind Infoline info@mind.org.uk 0300 123 3393

Information on a range of topics including:
- types of mental health problems
- where to get help
- medication and alternative treatments
- advocacy

Mind will look for details of help and support in your own area.

The National Association for People Abused in Childhood (NAPAC)
0808 801 0331 (freephone from landline and mobiles)
napac.org.uk
A charity supporting adult survivors of any form of childhood abuse.
Provides a support line and local support services.

NCT 0300 330 0700 nct.org.uk
National charity providing information and support for all parents.
National Institute for Health and Clinical Excellence (NICE)
nice.org.uk
Guidelines on treatments for depression.

No Panic www.nopanic.org.uk
No Panic are the people to call if you are suffering from panic attacks,
OCD, phobias, and other related anxiety disorders.
Helpline: **0844 967 4848** (Daily 10:00 – 22:00 Charges apply)
Youth Helpline for 13 - 20 yr olds: **0330 606 1174** (Mon - Fri 15:00 – 18:00
Charges apply)
Having a panic attack? Crisis number with recording of a breathing
technique: **01952 680835 (24 hr)**
Email: admin@nopanic.org.uk

NHS Choices nhs.uk
Provides information on treatments for depression available through
the NHS.

OCD Action www.ocdaction.org.uk 0845 390 6232 (Mon - Fri 09:30 - 17:00)
Support for people with OCD

Papyrus (Prevention of Young Suicide) www.papyrus-uk.org
Confidential advice and support for young people who feel suicidal.

- HOPELineUK: 0800 068 41 41

- Text: 07786 209 697

- Email: pat@papyrus-uk.org

Rethink Mental Illness www.rethink.org

0300 5000 927 (Mon – Fri 09:30 – 16:00)

Offers support and advice for people living with mental health issues

Samaritans

Chris, PO Box 9090, Stirling FK8 2SA Helpline: 116 123

jo@samaritans.org samaritans.org

A 24-hour telephone helpline for people struggling to cope.

Sane www.sane.org.uk

0300 304 7000 (4:30 – 10:30 every day)

A leading UK mental health charity

The Mix www.themix.org.uk

If you're under 25 you can talk to The Mix for free on the phone, by email or on their webchat. You can also use their phone counselling service, or get more information on support services you might need.

Freephone: 0808 808 4994 (13:00-23:00 daily)

Young Minds www.youngminds.org.uk

0808 802 5544 (Mon – Fri 09:30 – 16:00)

A helpline for parents on child and adolescent mental health

Youth Access www.youthaccess.org.uk

A place for you to get advice and information about counselling in the UK, if you're aged 12-25.

About the Author

Rachel Munns is a qualified counsellor, mindfulness practitioner and mental health first aider. She has worked with young people all over the UK for over a decade aiming to improve the mental wellbeing of the nation! She is a mum of two amazing teenage boys, wife of a wonderful hubby and general skivvy for her beautiful dog, Molly.

It is her greatest wish that no teenager should ever have to suffer the way her eldest son did, and this book is her way of sharing all the advice she possibly can to help others avoid the same difficulties. It is her hope that, through the simplicity of the Big Top Model and the Daily Workout, young people will find a way to navigate the challenges of their teenage years.

Rachel is a graduate of the Circus of Life.

Introducing Resilient Me

Rachel and Tony Munns are partners in Resilient Me, a company that provides a variety of services and resources that promote mental health awareness and resilience strategies.

There are a number of options for our presenters to deliver training courses at places of work, at schools, as 1:1 coaching and at open events taking place throughout the country. These include The Circus of Life, Brilliant Me and Prepare to Pass – more information and downloadable factsheets can be found on our website. New courses are being developed constantly, and you can track all the latest news and developments through our social media channels below.

As well as *The Circus of Life*, we have also published our own Positivity Journal, a full colour 200-page hardback book containing a positive thought for each day, plus space for all your notes and your daily workout (see pages 111-112).

The Journal is available to buy from the Resilient Me website or from Etsy *(just search Resilient Me Positivity Journal)*.

We really hope you have enjoyed and benefited from reading this book, and will keep in touch with Resilient Me to keep building your resilience and understanding of mental health issues for the future.

resilientme
resilientme.co.uk

f facebook.com/resilientmeuk   in linkedin.com/in/rachel-munns-resilientme

PUBLISHING

ISBN 9781916038004

01195

9 781916 038004